# THE BOOK OF CAIN

The Bible, as Bill Cain reminds us, is largely made up of family stories—stories of birth and death, of generations and legacies, joys and losses—with the astonishing claim that in these stories God is telling us a sacred story. What makes us think that story ended 2,000 years ago?

In this moving account of the months he spent caring for his mother through the ordeal following a diagnosis of terminal cancer, he shows us all how to add "a new book to the family Bible." With humor, affection, self-awareness, and his skills as a prize-winning playwright, Father Cain invites us to consider the ways that God's story is written in all the everyday dramas of family life—especially those that open our hearts, teach us to give and let go, and remind us what it means to be human.

**Bill Cain** is a Jesuit priest and acclaimed playwright, who co-created the television series "Nothing Sacred." He is author of *The Diary of Jesus Christ* (Orbis 2021).

# THE BOOK OF CAIN

*On Adding a New Book to the Family Bible*

Bill Cain, SJ

ORBIS BOOKS
**Maryknoll, New York 10545**

Founded in 1970, Orbis Books endeavors to publish works that enlighten the mind, nourish the spirit, and challenge the conscience. The publishing arm of the Maryknoll Fathers and Brothers, Orbis seeks to explore the global dimensions of the Christian faith and mission, to invite dialogue with diverse cultures and religious traditions, and to serve the cause of reconciliation and peace. The books published reflect the views of their authors and do not represent the official position of the Maryknoll Society. To learn more about Maryknoll and Orbis Books, please visit our website at www.orbisbooks.com

Manufactured in the United States of America

Library of Congress Cataloging-in-Publication Data

Names: Cain, Bill, 1947- author.
Title: The Book of Cain : on adding a new book to the family Bible / Bill Cain, S.J.
Description: Maryknoll, NY : Orbis Books, [2023] | Summary: "Priest and playwright Bill Cain offers a chronicle of the death of his mother, which, like book in the Bible, shows God's presence in the everyday dramas of ordinary families"— Provided by publisher.
Identifiers: LCCN 2022034938 (print) | LCCN 2022034939 (ebook) | ISBN 9781626985032 (trade paperback) | ISBN 9781608339655 (epub)
Subjects: LCSH: Bible—Criticism, interpretation, etc.
Classification: LCC BS511.3 .C34 2023 (print) | LCC BS511.3 (ebook) | DDC 220.6—dc23/eng/20221007
LC record available at https://lccn.loc.gov/2022034938
LC ebook record available at https://lccn.loc.gov/2022034939

*For*

*Nancy Marie Cain*

# Contents

# Foreword

## by Gregory Boyle

One of the many magnets that adorn our refrigerator in my Jesuit community is one of Jesus preaching the Sermon on the Mount. It is a pious, 1950s illustration of Jesus addressing the throngs on the hillside. Jesus says: "Okay everyone. Now listen carefully. I don't want to end up with four different versions of this."

We're afraid of "versions." We think they will take us down some Rashomon rabbit hole, and somehow, we won't know the truth, what really happened. But I say: Multiple books, continuing stories, endless versions, bring 'em on! They only enhance what is luminous, spacious, and reveal the expansive heart of God. Bill Cain's book welcomes it all as the "law and the prophets." When it comes to "versions," Bill is fearless. Everything belongs. The welcome mat is there for every story and version of that story.

This book needs no introduction.

Every morning, my spiritual director, a homie named Sergio, and I, exchange emails about the day's readings. He often talks about the "mystical lens" that needs to filter things out, the stuff in the Bible you just don't buy. I call it "finding the invitation." Otherwise, we get tripped up by a wrathful God or distracted by Jesus thinking the guy with epilepsy is possessed by a demon. Or maybe we just can't get past the king who invites folks from the highways and byways to the feast, only to have the man who is inappropriately dressed taken outside and beaten. Find the invitation. What are we being invited to? Well, it's a banquet. Focus on that. Use your mystical lens. There's always an invitation in it. God doesn't indict. God invites. Like the tired joke Ronald Reagan always told about the pile of horse manure, "There has to be a pony in here somewhere." Use the mystical filter and find the invitation.

Over these many years of knowing and living in community with Bill Cain, I had read or heard parts of this tender book before. But I read the entire "Book of Cain" (On Adding a New Book to the Family Bible) on a plane. I kind of don't recommend that. I was traveling with two gang members from Homeboy Industries. I laughed and cried so many times, the homie next to me started to get worried. As I read, I "found the invitation" to generosity, flourishing joy, and a longing to hold and to be held, gently. The homie next to me, a first-time flyer, was annoyed as I kept reading, especially during some rough turbulence. "Why are you not freaking out by this?" When we had something of a screechingly hard landing in Los Angeles (and had we not been seat-belted, we would have ended up in the laps of the folks in the row ahead of us), he turns to me and deadpans: "I did not like our driver."

Bill Cain's book invited me, all over again, to delight in this present moment and to discover (anew) that who we are IS loving attention. The essence of revelation is to find the revealing as it still happens. It didn't stop 2000 years ago, as Bill Cain insists. What is revealed in the present moment is eternally replenishing and inviting us to cherish. Choosing to cherish with every breath is not hard. Remembering to cherish...now that's difficult.

This book reminds us to remember.

It needs no introduction.

On February 27, 1544, Ignatius of Loyola enters a word, in his spiritual journal, for the very first time. He proceeds to use this word a lot for the twelve years remaining in his life. Before he dies, he goes back and circles this word. Now, I speak Spanish, but I had never heard of this word before. The word is *Acatamiento*. It comes from a somewhat archaic word, "Acatar" which means "to look at something with attention." It would sometimes be used, in the time of Ignatius, to speak of one's delight in being asked by the King to do something. And one would be thrilled to look at this task with attention. It gets translated in English as "affectionate awe." Surely, this was all reflective of a private, mystical moment between Ignatius and the God who, as he says, "is always greater." But at the end of his life, Ignatius didn't settle for a "moment," but held out for a movement. I don't mean the Society of Jesus. "Affectionate awe" was a stance in the world. For Ignatius, it was his mystical lens. It came to him, with clarity, in the last years of his life. Adding a new book to the Bible happens when we "find God in all things," as Ignatius would say, and delight in what we find there. Or by knowing that God is still speaking, that the font of revelation is "not closed...but close," as Bill Cain would say.

On the page, on the stage, in person, Bill Cain is good company. But really, this book keeps you company. It keeps you connected to the wholeness you long for. It untethers your aloneness and brings you in to beloved belonging. It keeps you company while, at the same time, you find comfort in your story, in your version of things. It finds the tender core of your true self in loving. It replaces the narrative you cling to, the version that floats your boat and keeps it from taking water, and, instead, you're invited to your own story, which is different from the narrative you've come to believe. Bill Cain reminds you to remember that no part of your story is untouched by God's yearning to be intimate. Our stance is "affectionate awe," and we are reminded that this is God's stance with our stories as well.

These pages kept me company and drew me closer to the God who loves us without measure and without regret. But it also held an invitation to the story beyond the narrative. It drew me into a profound desire to look at my story with "attention." *Acatamiento*. Adding books, tagging another chapter, welcoming as many versions of revelation as can be cherished. Endless.

This book needs no introduction.

# On Adding a New Book to the Bible

### God: The Complete Works

Can someone please tell me why the Bible ends?

I understand why *The Complete Works of Shakespeare* ends. Shakespeare died. No more Shakespeare, no more Works.

But the Bible?

The Bible is a dialogue we've been having with God for millennia. A tag team of authors have added to it whenever we—or God—have had something new to say.

God's still here; we're still here.

Who decided the conversation was over?

I remember asking a priest when I was in grammar school why the Bible ended. He told me, "The font of revelation has been closed." I wondered at the time, "What fool closed it?"

The last new book in any version of the Bible—Jewish or Christian—was written by roughly 100 AD. We would never accept the limits of the science, medicine or—God forbid—the plumbing from two millennia ago, so why do we accept without question the limits of revelation at that time?

Who stopped the clock on God?

Who decided that—by the year 100—God had written *God: The Complete Works?*

———

I suppose we should be grateful the Bible doesn't end any earlier than it does. If it had stopped at Exodus, what a loss not to have known David. If it had stopped at David, how sad not to have known Isaiah. If it had stopped at the prophets, what a tragedy not to have known Jesus. Stopping where it does, I wonder: What, as a result, have we missed?—because the Bible was going somewhere when it stopped, but it stopped before it got there. This is true whether your Bible ends with the prophets dreaming of a holy mountain where all people can live together in peace or with Jesus trying to realize that vision. The vision at the heart of the Bible can be expressed as a simple riddle. A magnificent, unapproachable God says to us, "Approach. Come closer...."

*Closer* is the impulse behind every book in the Bible.

And we were getting there.

Maybe not *close* yet, but *closer.*

And then the book ends, leaving out the last two thousand years of the story.

Because ultimately, that's what the Bible is....

A book of stories.

I know people keep trying to turn it into a rule book, but I wonder if the people who think of the Bible as a rule book have actually ever *read* it. Admittedly, it has Ten Commandments and they tell us who we are *supposed* to be, but it has tens of thousands of stories that tell us who we actually are and, in all the best stories, the commandments are repeatedly and enthusiastically broken. For some reason—call it the Prodigal Son factor—God seems to love the stories of people who break his commandments more than those of the ones who keep them. What a shame, then, that the book ends, because the story of God's many prodigal sons and daughters goes on. It goes on in you. Your story matters. It matters to God. I suppose this is the most basic form of faith. Believing your story actually matters.

———

I was eighteen years old and studying for the priesthood when I first read the Bible cover to cover.

Since I was raised Catholic, the Bible had not been a prominent part of my growing up. After all, we had the catechism and the catechism had the definitive answers to all of life's significant questions. *Question:* Who is God? *Answer:* God is the Creator of heaven and earth, and of all things. *Question:* Why did God make you? *Answer:* God made me to know Him, to love Him, and to serve Him in this world, and to be happy with Him forever in heaven.

The great riddles of life solved on the first page of the catechism!

Fortunately, a theology professor, appalled at his seminarians' ignorance of the Bible, sat us down and had us read it—Genesis to Apocalypse—and it was...well...a revelation.

The first and most wonderful learning—at which I continue to rejoice—was that revelation isn't a catechism to be memorized.

It is a story to be lived.

Yes, certain thorny problems arose. For one, science had clearly outpaced revelation. What does one do about that? For another, can the last word on slavery possibly be St. Paul's "Slaves, be obedient to your masters"? And how can a book that claims to be the fullness of revelation contain not a single word written by a woman? The problems multiply as you read on ...

But the Bible had this going for it:

God was not a detached deity sitting on Olympus unconcerned. Or some woodland nymph occupied only by the cycle of the seasons. God was intimately involved in the story of this human, flawed, frequently dysfunctional, nearly always prodigal family.

If you want to see God—says the Book—look at your family's story.

———

The moment that awakened me to how much God cares about his family was when I read Genesis, chapter 23. The death of Abraham's wife, Sarah. Her death shocked me. I should have been prepared—she was, after all, 127 years old—but I had fallen in love with her a few chapters earlier. God had just promised that, even though she was 80, Sarah would have the child she and Abraham had always longed for. This is the sacred promise on which the whole Bible is founded, and what was her reaction?

Sarah laughed.

She wasn't saying no to God. She was game. She just thought the whole thing was preposterous. Which it was. Her laughter makes even God stop and ask, "Is anything too wonderful for God?"

God was passionately interested in Sarah. If you haven't noticed this before she dies, you will with her death, because, when Sarah dies, Genesis, that runaway train of a story, comes to an absolute halt. It doesn't have to. She has played her part. She is no longer important to the narrative. But, suddenly, everything stops.

All of chapter 23 in Genesis is devoted to Sarah's funeral arrangements—the same amount of space that the Bible devotes to the creation of the universe. Four millennia later, we still know the minutiae of her burial—the buying of the plot, the land, the cave, the trees. She mattered. This one individual woman—with her crazy, adventurous life—mattered. Four millennia later, we are still telling her story.

I am grateful to her family for saving her story—and her husband's. And their children's stories. I am grateful to the friends of Jesus who saved not just one, but four versions of his life for us. How easy it would have been to lose the story of this carpenter whose memory Rome tried to erase. My parents gave me these stories and entrusted them to me to pass on as they had been passed on to them by their parents. And, speaking of parents—

My own parents—at this moment—are turning into stories.

A priest now myself, I have said both of their funerals— my mother's only days ago. And now my parents are turning into stories. As I will before too long. You too.

I want to believe this matters. All of it. The joy and the pain. The love and the loss. The glory of the Ark and the suffering of the cross. I want to believe that the before and the after and the transition in between matter. In the last few days I have heard hundreds of stories about my mother and father. Some that I had never heard before. This surprises me because I thought I knew all the stories. My mom and dad were, each in a different way, gifted storytellers. Neighbors use to come to sit at this kitchen table just to hear them talk. I want to believe there was revelation in their stories. Not only a repetition of old truths. But something new. Something surprising. Something of God. I want to believe that, in their journeys, their private sacraments, the rituals unique to them, there was revelation, just as there was in Sarah's laughter.

I want to discover and claim that revelation.

I want to write a new book for the Bible.

And so...

I make a quiet vow here alone at the kitchen table, where I sat with my mother just a few days ago. In the next year I will honor my parents' stories as Abraham and Sarah's children did theirs As Jesus's friends did his. Together their lives spanned most of a century. As best I can, I will sift through a hundred years of stories, always looking for what God chose to reveal in the lives of two perfectly ordinary, absolutely extraordinary people—Pete Cain and Mary Dawson. A new book. Non-canonical perhaps, but nonetheless revelatory. And perhaps, in doing so, I might be able to find a way to keep the story that began with Abraham and Sarah going forward. A way to continue to claim the revelation that comes our way.

Perhaps—every hundred years or so—*every* family can be invited to submit a book of their stories, the stories of their journey with God through the events, large and small, of their time. And, if *every* family's entry cannot be added to *everyone's* Bible, perhaps—every hundred years—each family can add a new book to the family Bible. Until finally, come the Last Judgment, the book will be complete.

———

First, of course, if we wish to complete the Book, we will have to catch up with the past two thousand years. It shouldn't be that difficult, because it's not that we haven't been writing about our relationship with God endlessly. We are spoiled for choices. I think with twenty additional books—one for every hundred years or so—we ought to be able to fulfill our obligation of catching up with the story. Nominations are open. If you could pick a book—any book—that described our continuing conversation with God at any point during the last two thousand years—a book not already included in the Bible—which one would you choose?

My personal choice for a book to represent the last hundred years from existing literature would be by a woman—a young woman—Anne Frank.

Her *Diary*, like the Bible, is a family story. It is a small story, confined within a tiny labyrinth of rooms on top of 263 Prinsengracht in Amsterdam. But, like the Pentateuch and the Gospels, it reveals on every page the inexhaustible depth of a human soul. And, at the same time, it reveals just how much revelation we still need.

———

For now, please accept the following submission on behalf of my family.

The Book of Cain.

I look forward to reading yours.

— Bill Cain, SJ

## Chapter 1. On Adding a New Book to the Bible

Where does the story of your family begin?

My own family has a very short memory. My parents never knew their grandparents who were left behind in an old world—which sounds very biblical. And, since my parents married late, I never knew my grandparents. A loss.

Your family? A long memory or short?

Before we gather stories for the family Bible, take time to remember.

And remember that the Bible as we have it is a second draft. Before it was written in words, it was written in meals and journeys, in births and deaths.

Your ancestors certainly saw times of peace and prosperity, wars and depressions, times of stability and times of migration—exactly the same as our ancestors in biblical times.

What are the stories that have been saved and passed down to you?

What stories of faith? What stories of despair?

Like the writers of the Bible, what stories do you choose to pass on to the next generation?

## 2

# *Revelation*

---

Where do you start when writing a new book for the Bible?

"In the beginning" has been taken.

Twice.

Once in Genesis (*In the beginning God created heaven and earth...*) and once in John (*In the beginning was the Word...*)

Where to start?

Faced with the epic journeys of the Bible—passing though seas or walking across them, wandering forty years in a desert or spending forty days there wrestling with the devil—I'm intimidated. Who takes those kinds of journeys?

I think the true answer—the biblical answer—is: we all do. Some journeys are more visibly dramatic than others, but each journey through life is an infinite one and even the meekest among us have to deal with a final, ultimate adventure—death. So, in the search for a verse to begin, let's start there. I will start with the events surrounding the announcement of my mother's death as the beginning of a journey.

I will look for a verse that is memorable. Compassionate, empathetic, bold, courageous. As it is revelation I am looking for, I will look for something surprising. Above all,

I will look for something simple. Something as simple as my two favorite verses from the Bible.

"Sarah laughed" and "Jesus wept."

————

Thinking back on that beautiful, leaves-are-changing October, I can think of five things that people said, each of which could be a good starting verse. But which?

1. *"Can I watch the playoffs now?"*

2. *"Well, you do what you can."*

3. *"We found it by mistake, Mary."*

4. *"Time to finally grow up."*

5. *"Mary, from now on, our main concern is your dignity and your comfort."*

Each has its own story.

————

### 1. *"Can I watch the playoffs now?"*
#### OCTOBER 9

*Mary Cain.*
My mother's name is called and we go in to see Dr. T.

My mother had been having back pains and her doctor—Dr. P—had sent her to a surgeon—Dr. T—to investigate the cause of the pain. My mother worships young, vital, handsome Dr. P. Consequently, she went through all the tests that Dr. T—a stereotypically cold surgeon—had set up for her in an icy visit two weeks ago. We are here in Dr. T's office today for the results.

We face Dr. T across his desk. He sits in front of a wall of diplomas. On the desk there is a pile of folders. Each folder a life. The doctor is smiling. Good news, I wonder?

He waits. We wait. And then he asks pleasantly— *Yes, and what can I do for you?*

He has absolutely no conception of who we are and this makes me angry, because for the past two weeks we have thought of nothing but him and his tests. I say, annoyed and letting it show, "We're here for the results."

The doctor says, "Of?"

Mom, sensing my anger rising, puts a hand on my arm and takes over. She says, "The results of the tests, Doctor."

The doctor says, "Tests?"

I want to attack the doctor, but Mom continues pleasantly, "We saw you two weeks ago, Doctor. My doctor—Dr. Polycarp—sent me to you to find out what's causing the pain in my back. You ordered tests, Doctor. Oh Doctor, I drank a gallon of the worst tasting—"

The doctor remembers. "Ah, yes. You had lost some blood. We thought it might be your new heart valves. Your name?"

"Mary Cain, Doctor. And the valves aren't new, doctor, I've had them twenty years." As he searches through his files he asks, "What kind did they give you?"

"Pig," Mary says.

"Twenty years? Pig valves don't usually last that long."

"Well, doctor," Mary says, "this was evidently an exceptional pig."

The doctor says, "I can't find your file. Would you mind waiting in the hall?"

My mother rises with difficulty saying, "No problem, Doctor," but before we are out of the room he says, "Oh, here it is." He looks at the file. Head in the file, he says blandly, "There are inoperable lesions on the liver."

He looks up with a small smile.

Though very smart, Mary Cain does not realize that her death sentence has just been read. She doesn't pick up information unless there is emotional content attached to it and the blasé tone of the doctor's casual "lesions on the liver" didn't register as terribly important.

I say, "Doctor, could I speak with you alone for a moment?"

So, while Mom had blood drawn, I talk with the doctor privately. *Aggressive chemotherapy can slow the progression.* ... Knowing my mother, at her age, would never go for that, I ask for the prognosis. *Well, six months is the usual number, but that doesn't mean anything really.* Another name is called and the conversation is over.

As we leave, Mom asks, "Well, what was that all about?"

I lie and say, "He says you need more tests."

"Oh no, Billy, not *more* tests!"

I don't tell Mom then that she is going to die.

I know I will be leaving Syracuse for New York City, my home, in a day or two. I don't want to announce, "You're dying" and then leave her alone with the news. Better go to New York, get what I need, pack my bags, come back to Syracuse and say, "I'm here. I will see you through."

I was back from New York within the week. It took me another week to tell her. I explained the delay to myself by saying the time was never right, but the truth was I just couldn't bring myself to do it. Finally—

### OCTOBER 18

I ask Mom to turn off the post-season baseball game that she is watching on television.

She says, "But it's the playoffs."

I sit down next to her on the couch.

Mom gets a suspicious look and turns off the television.

I quietly break the news to Mom. I tell her why I haven't told her before. Tell her all I know except for what the doctor said was meaningless—six months to live.

She is silent for a long time.

Then she speaks.

Seriously, but easily.

*Thank you, Billy, for telling me so kindly.*

I try to explain. *I didn't tell you before because.... Well, because.*

She nods and says, *I sort of knew.*

I say, *I didn't think you understood "lesions on the liver."*

She gives a small laugh and continues, *I didn't. But still.*

I ask, *How did you know?*

She says, *The doctor. He wouldn't look at me.*

Amused, she continues, *And he did his best to lose the file. He's a nice man, Billy, just ...frightened.*

I ask, *Well, what do you think?*

She pauses. Then—*Well, it seems like a shame to have gone through all this pain and still not get better.*

She is quiet again. Then—

*Thank you for your kindness.*

Then—

*I'll do the best I can.*

Then—

*I'll offer it up.*

Then she is quiet for a long time.

And I sit there wondering what she is thinking.

Then, having been faced with the news of her own death, she looks me straight in the eye and asks, *Can I watch the playoffs now?*

———

*Can I watch the playoffs now?* as a response to a death sentence? I submit that this will be a hard line to beat for courage.

————

## 2. "Well, you do what you can."

*Mary, take that thing off.*

Mom didn't cry over the diagnosis. Neither did any of the small band of my mother's friends—all women, all over sixty-five, all frighteningly energetic. Paulette, my favorite (and the most energetic of the bunch), did not cry. She would do in the face of the death of her friend what she has done every day of her life. *You do the best you can. What else can you do?*

Paulette's sorrow and anger at the impending death of her friend (and all that energy) found their focus in a ratty, torn old robe that my mother had been wearing continually since she had gotten sick. I had tried to do something about the robe—I had even threatened calling the EPA about it— but I could never get the damn thing off her. *It belonged to Cathy's mother and it's comfortable.*

The first we saw of Paulette after the news broke, she didn't have a thing to say about the diagnosis—no word of comfort, no tears. On the contrary. She stormed into the apartment, pointed at the ratty robe and commanded, *Mary, take that thing off.* Mary, startled, took the thing off immediately, excessively modest though she usually was, right there in the living room. Paulette produced a JC Penney's bag, took out a new robe, put it on Mom, put the old robe in the bag, put a jar of homemade applesauce in the fridge, and disappeared. The next day she reappeared with the ratty robe washed, pressed, patched, and rehemmed.

*I couldn't do a thing with the elbows, so I made the sleeves two-thirds length. So what can you do?*... Then Paulette put every ounce of her sorrow and anger at her friend's impending death into her feelings about that damn robe. *Well, what can you DO? You just do the BEST you CAN!*

———

Compassionate, empathetic, bold, and generous.

———

### 3. *I'm so sorry, Mary.*

Dr. P—Mom's primary—is young.

Mom was one of his first patients and she loves him. As he checks her vital signs, they talk about a fire engine the doctor bought for his son, a toy that he can play with only if he'll wear shorts instead of a diaper. Then, an embarrassed silence. Then Mom asks simply: *Is there anything...?*

As Dr. P speaks, he avoids meeting her eyes. Why? What is he afraid of seeing? Some accusation of failure? Unlikely. She worships him. And in any case, he needn't have worried. Mary was looking directly at the floor all the time he was looking directly at the wall. Then, *How long do I...?*

*Oh, Mary, there's no number we can put on it. Hell, I'm not sure you'd want one if we could. I mean, if they found out that I had cancer and it would affect me twenty years down the road, I'm not sure I'd want to know.* And, as good as he is, his perfect health disqualifies him from understanding her. This cancer isn't twenty years down the road. It's in the office—here, now. And Mom knows that even if he doesn't. Then he does a very surprising thing. He apologizes to my mother for finding her cancer. *We found it by mistake, Mary.*

*It was a mistake. We just came across it while we were looking for what was giving you all that back pain. I'm so sorry...*

Then, nearly apologizing, the young doctor repeats a wish he could unmake his discovery: *I'm so sorry, Mary, it was a mistake. We found it by mistake....*

———

A doctor's heart breaking for his patient.

———

### 4. *"Time to grow up."*

No two people have the same parents.

By the time I was born—three years after my older brother Paul—my parents had changed vastly from the people who had welcomed him into the world with unreasonable hopes and overwhelming expectations.

When I arrived, my parents were pretty much willing to let me be whoever I needed to be. My three-year-old big brother had broken them in for me by stubbornly refusing to be anybody but himself. And who was he? Well, put simply, he was not *them.*

My beautiful brother became himself by contraries. In direct contradiction to Mom's down-to-the-last-detail perfectionism, Paul became perfectly careless. In direct contradiction to Dad's easy-going nature, Paul became heroic. And, over time, my carelessly heroic big brother met and surpassed, at great cost, their hopes and expectations—always on his own terms, which were usually far more demanding than theirs.

God help first children.

Living in faraway El Paso with his wife and daughter, Paul didn't have the luxury of distracting himself with all the medical concerns that were keeping me preoccupied and protected. Paul received the news simply and he fell apart.

And what did my carelessly heroic big brother, decorated veteran, nationally recognized teacher, father of a family, say when he fell apart? The most grown-up person I know said, choking on his sorrow, *My last parent is dying. Time for me to grow up finally.*

————

Clearly the start of another journey.

————

### 5. *"Mary, from now on, our main concern is your dignity and your comfort."*

**OCTOBER 27**

*Mary Cain.*

This time Dr. T remembers her; this time Mom knows what is going on.

As Mom and he talk, I sit—silent and resentful—and watch Dr. T across his file-covered desk. Beyond the fact that I simply don't like him, I can't figure out why he made this appointment with us. He's a surgeon; the cancer is inoperable; there is no reason for us to be here. I haven't yet learned that doctors' appointments—like cancer itself—reproduce mindlessly. I didn't know that yet and, in retrospect, I'm glad I didn't.

Dr. T tells Mom there's nothing to add to what she already knows. From now on all care will be through Dr. P. The end. He closes her folder and moves it from one pile to another.

I am finding it hard to even be civil to Dr. T.

There is an awkward silence. It's my job at this point to say "Thank you, Doctor," but I don't.

Silence.

Then he says something.

Something very simple.

He says it honestly, warmly, and with supreme kindness.

This is followed by a brief pause.

Just for a moment, Mom smiles like a girl unexpectedly asked to dance, charmed by the doctor's words.

And then, for the first time since she heard the news weeks ago, she cries.

This surprises and embarrasses her, but the emotion behind the tears is huge and her embarrassment is no match for it.

Her tears seem to me very old.

How old?

Mary is eighty-one.

Her life has spanned most of a century.

Early in the century, Mary Dawson was born the daughter of a shanty Irish immigrant, Johanna Ryan Dawson. Johanna cleaned rich people's houses and took in their laundry after her young husband died (cancer). *I never knew him, Billy. I was three when he died...*

Mary, who started work—ironing—when she was seven to help her mother....

Mary, who got her first paying job the day she graduated from Vocational High in the middle of the Depression. *Not the day after, Billy. I worked that day and graduated that night.*

Mary, who worked job after job until she and Pete started their family. *More ironing, Billy. I used to do so many shirts for your father that there was no place to hang them all....*

Mary Cain, who, when she had to go back to work at forty-nine, was told by an employment agent, *But you're forty-nine!*, said, *So you better get me a job fast because I'm going to be fifty soon and think how much harder it will be then!*

Mrs. Cain, who doubled her salary in a year working in a factory, then moved into management and continued to work, and work hard, to take care of her husband (through a long life and a hard death), her sons, and her army of friends until just taking care of herself became a full-time job.

Mary, who has done a lifetime of hard work and who thought her death would be one more job in a lifetime of hard jobs, Mary is crying very old tears.

She is not crying because of her coming death, though the doctor could not know that. She is crying because this near-stranger is offering her something she has always wanted and no one, till now, has ever offered it to her.

What the doctor had said was, *"Mary, from now on, our main concern is your dignity and your comfort."*

———

Mary Cain, who has spent all of a hard-working life struggling for other people's dignity and comfort, is being offered her own. And she is finally too tired, too worn down, too sad, not to accept it.

And Mary cried.

And Sarah laughed.

And Jesus wept.

1. *"Can I watch the playoffs now?"*

2. *"I'm so sorry, Mary."*

3. *"Well, you do what you can."*

4. *"Time to finally grow up."*

5. *"Mary, from now on, our main concern is your dignity and your comfort."*

———

Much as I hate to vote against a line I cherish, *Can I watch the playoffs now?*, what the doctor said was really a revelation—and not just a revelation that Mom's death might offer her something that her life had not—as wonderfully hopeful as that was. The moment itself was a revelation. The doctor was a revelation. A revelation of the unexpected tenderness that lives deep within the most unexpected, most ordinary places where God waits, has always waited, always waits to be revealed.

———

As she rises to leave Dr. T and his files, she smiles.
   *Doctor, you've been very kind to me.*
   *Well, you're easy to be kind to.*
   *Oh, no. Not me. I'm nothing but trouble.*
   And we find our way to the door and begin a new journey.

### Chapter 2. Revelation

*And behold, the Lord passed by, and a great and strong wind
rent the mountains, and broke in pieces the rocks before the
Lord, but the Lord was not in the wind; and after the wind an
earthquake, but the Lord was not in the earthquake; and after the
earthquake a fire, but the Lord was not in the fire; and after the
fire a still small voice ...*

—*1 Kings 19:11–12*

God was not in the storm or the earthquake or the fire.
God appeared in a small still voice. Simple words mark
great changes.

"Do you take this man ...? This woman ...?" "I do."

"What name do you give the child?"

Small statements with momentous consequences.

In the Gospels, some of the most earth-shaking moments
are surprisingly quiet ones.

"Let it be done to me according to your word."

"Follow me."

"They have no wine."

"This is my body."

And the world was changed and God entered in a new way.

What simple words are remembered by your family?

In the quiet of memory, what small still voices speak?

# 3
# *Sacrament*

---

OCTOBER 31
*Many years before*

I wasn't supposed to be born on Halloween.

I arrived haphazardly on the scene—five weeks premature—when Mom's water broke in the produce section of the grocery store. Dad ran home from work to find our neighbor, Molly, hanging out the second-floor apartment window shouting, *Pete, get a cab.* So Pete ran up to Queens Boulevard and got a cab, but when the cab driver got a look at my mother in labor, he said no way was she getting in his cab.

My father, normally a peaceful man, started a fight with him and the driver came back at him with a tire iron at which point Molly shouted from the window again, *For Christ's sake, Pete, there are other cabs!* And that was my introduction to the world.

And my first Halloween.

———

Halloween.

Even as an adult, Halloween remains a time for pure celebration, one of the few remaining no-pressure holidays. And as a kid, wow! Grown-ups were standing behind every door just waiting to give you the candy you had to beg for any other day. It was pure joy.

Most years.

———

I have no idea how old I was—somewhere between six and ten, I suppose.

In any case, I was old enough to go with Dad, the day before Halloween, to help pick out the pumpkin and, this year, to carry it home from the store.

Now the pumpkin was always a big deal in our house, and carrying it home was a major honor. I don't think even my big brother was ever allowed to do that, though he was allowed to carry the thin end of the Christmas tree back from the boulevard with dad carrying the heavy end.

But, for me, the pumpkin was better than any Christmas tree.

For one thing, there was that great shock of orange, which sort of matched my hair (and personality) as a child. Then, sitting with dad as he took out his draftsman's tools (a draftsman and engineer by trade) to draw the face on the pumpkin. *How many teeth, boys? Scary or smiling?* Then the candle flickering inside giving it life, changing its expression. Oh, yeah, I'd take a pumpkin over a Christmas tree any day.

(Besides, the folks never fought about carving the pumpkin the way they battled over trimming the tree. Mom's one-strand-of-tinsel-at-a-time technique always brought out the anarchist in Dad and the fight was on. My brother and I still can't look at a Christmas tree without a slight feeling of dread.)

In any case, this year I got to pick the pumpkin and carry it home.

I remember it was a stunning autumn day and the neighbors were all out from their cramped, overcrowded apartments on the front stoops, fire escapes, window sills. It must have been a Saturday. In memory the day has the joyous freedom of a Saturday morning with the whole weekend ahead. I could feel my father's pride in me shining on my back as he walked behind me and the pumpkin, stopping to talk with the Biettas or the Sullivans—

*Yes, growing up, getting big, another birthday, quite a boy. Come to the party tomorrow. The more the merrier and Mary'll love to see you.*

Simple, deep, contented, childhood happiness.

And then—

I dropped the pumpkin.

With everyone watching, the pumpkin—and, with it, my world and my sense of self—smashed into a million pieces.

———

I ran.

Ran as fast as I could into our apartment building, up the dark stairs, into the apartment, past my mother, and into my bedroom. I slammed the door, threw myself down on the bed and sobbed my heart out.

All attempts to reassure me that this wasn't the end of the world were unsuccessful. Offers of new pumpkins, refused. I was deeply ashamed. I didn't want a party the next day. No! I didn't want lunch and later I didn't want dinner. *Well, what do you want, Billy?* I just wanted to be left alone. For the rest of my life.

I had dropped the pumpkin. I had smashed the world to bits. I remember lying there, inconsolable, sobbing on the bed.

I must have slept through the afternoon, through the twilight, because the next thing I remember is waking up in a dark room.

Into the darkness came my father.

He was carrying a perfectly carved jack-o'-lantern.

*Take it away. Take it away. Take it away. I don't want this pumpkin. I broke my pumpkin. I don't want another one.*

But this wasn't another one.

*Billy, this is your pumpkin.*

This was, in fact, my pumpkin.

*Really?*

And he answered confidently, quietly, sure of himself.

*Really, Billy. I wouldn't lie to you.*

And he wouldn't. Wouldn't know how.

After the disaster, my father, seeing how upset I was, went back into the street, collected the pieces of the shattered pumpkin, and brought them home.

Then, while I was crying in the bedroom, dad (draftsman and engineer by trade) carefully rebuilt the pumpkin. Like a carpenter of old, he used toothpicks to hold the whole thing together. Then, once it was back in shape, he carved a face into it, complete with the big gap-toothed smile and, when the darkness was complete, he put a candle in it and brought it into my room.

And, in the dark, it was beautiful.

I couldn't admit this, of course. I had committed far too deeply to my own unhappiness to give it up by this point— *Take it away, take it away, take it away*—but my father was unfazed by my unhappiness.

He placed the pumpkin, candle burning inside, on the windowsill. Then he sat on the side of my bed as he did many nights when he would rub my back and sing me to sleep. No songs tonight, though. He put a hand on my back and said quietly:

*Billy, you'll have a lot of birthdays in your life. And you'll have a lot of pumpkins. But you know what?*

*What?*

*Out of all the pumpkins you'll ever have, this is the only one you'll ever remember.*

———

And then he left me alone with the only pumpkin I ever have remembered.

Broken.

Reassembled with love.

Grinning and shining brightly in the dark.

———

### OCTOBER 31
### *This year*

This year my birthday was very quiet.

Friends called, but it was just my mother and myself, alone in an apartment in Syracuse, New York.

A few days earlier, I had told her she was dying.

It's all a little lonely.

As Mom goes to bed, she stops at my room and says, *Good night, Billy. And happy birthday.*

*Thank you, Mom. Good night.*

Then, after a silence,

*Sorry.*

*For what?*

*Oh, that I couldn't do more for your birthday.*

*You did fine. I wouldn't be having a birthday if it weren't for you.*

Silence. Then, with a laugh.

*My water broke in the supermarket.*

*I know.*

*Your father almost got in a fight with the cab driver.*

A shake of the head, a shared laugh, a shared silence. Then, an exchange that has become ritual over the years—

*Thank you for having me.*

*The pleasure was all mine. . . . Happy Birthday, Billy.*

*Good night, Mom.*

Shuffle, shuffle, shuffle.

Silence.

Darkness.

And the memory of a pumpkin—broken, reassembled with love, grinning and shining bravely in the dark—explaining all of life to me.

### Chapter 3. Sacrament

*"Those who cannot remember the past are condemned to repeat it."*
—*George Santayana*

Yes, forgetting the past may force us to repeat it.

Even so, there are some events from the past that we choose to repeat just so we can remember them.

Easter. Passover.

We re-enact every year events of such magnitude that we wish to live again within the experience of our ancestors.

Some of these re-enactments are once in a lifetime events, like baptism.

Others are constantly recurring, such as sacraments of forgiveness and Eucharist.

We had seven official sacraments, but an endless stream of other informal ceremonies that recalled events personal to our family.

Minor sacraments of our love.

I can't look at a carved pumpkin without being in the presence of my father.

What events are minor sacraments of your family?

What unrepeatable events are called to mind by meals, conversations, ceremonies, times of year?

# 4

# *The Six Commandments*

All families have rules.

Rules are the deals you make with one another to hold the family together. Not all families have their rules engraved on stone tablets, but then again, not all families are as wildly dysfunctional as the family in the Bible.

Families make the rules they need, and your family's rules tell you something essential about the nature of your family.

The Ten Commandments give us an idea of the vast range of passions that needed to be controlled among the children of Abraham and Sarah, Isaac and Rebecca, and Jacob and—well—Rachel, Leah, Zilpah, and Bilhah.

All families have rules.

Though ours were unspoken, I think my family had six. I have checked them out with my brother and he says they are, more or less, correct.

*All* of them are rules for fights.

I want to say something about my family that I have never heard anybody say about theirs. I feel I am taking a risk by saying it, but here it is:

I come from a functional family.

*Fine,* I hear you say, *if your family was so functional, how come the fights?*

All families fight.

A functional family fights fair.
We were functional as hell and we fought like pros.

### Rules for Family Fights

**Rule #2.**
Fights between parents were never physical; fights
between kids, in general, should not result in stitches.

**Rule #3.**
Fights between parents were the parents' business;
fights between kids, the kids' business.

**Rule #4.**
Nobody cares what the neighbors think.

**Rule #5.**
Extremes of feeling were allowed, especially kids to
adults. And you could say *anything*. Kids could say to
parents *I hate you* without fear of retaliation. Of
course you hated them some of the time. They were
your parents.

**Rule #6.**
You didn't go to bed without saying good night to
everybody. You could sulk, but you said good night.

Which leaves Rule #1.

I have saved it for last because it was, without question,
the most important.

**Rule #1:**
Nobody walks out on a fight.
Nobody.

Nobody storms out.

Nobody runs away.

You fight until the fight is over.

Through the shouting, beyond the tears, sometimes past the point of exhaustion, but, until you arrived at a solution, nobody leaves the room.

———

We weren't *always* able to fight fair. Cornered, people struck out. That, too, was understood, though it left scars.

———

Still, the fights that tore at us never tore us apart.

In a way that I find hard to explain to friends, and perhaps I won't be able to explain here either, these fights, painful as they were, brought us together. They were painful, in fact, because they brought us together. They brought us together at the exact point where we were most raw, most unloved, and most nearly unlovable. But still, somehow, together.

It was always understood, regardless of any fight's outcome, that we would still be together after. (That's why you always had to say good night to everyone—see Rule #6.) Knowing that nothing could tear us apart, we were free to battle honestly to the solution of whatever was bothering us.

Except...

———

Except when there *was* no solution to what was bothering us.

These fights, probably one a year, always between parents, left scars on us all that lasted a lifetime. Maybe beyond.

As a child I thought of my parents as just that, my parents, an undividable unity. But a fight with no solution made it clear that they were a unit only by agreement. These annual fights revealed to me as a child the fundamental, unhealable rift that exists between any two people, the terrifying loneliness of the individuals who make up a couple, the unavoidable individuality of my parents.

They gave me the first recurring nightmare that I can remember.

An enormous rock rolls down a mountain, gathering speed as it goes. It must be stopped or disaster will occur. The only thing in its path is a thin golden wire. Can the wire stop the boulder? And I wake up crying.

The boulder was my mother's rage; the golden wire was my father's patience.

———

### My Father and the Door

My father.

The worst thing anybody ever said about my father was said first by Uncle Dick and was then repeated over a lifetime by others in a variety of situations.

*Well,* said Dick about my father, *Pete always was a good dancer.*

Context in this case means everything.

———

Young Pete Cain was a classy dresser.

*Billy, you could cut bread with the crease in Pete's pants—* and this in spite of the fact that he was working pick-and-shovel at the time. He didn't have money, but he did have five brothers all pretty much the same size and the rule was *First up, best dressed.* What pick-and-shovel money Pete did have went into buying a new Ford in which he courted Mary Dawson who was dirt poor but also a classy dresser thanks to a mother who could sew and alcoholic Aunt Lala—*She never drank during the day, Billy*—who worked at Chappell's department store and got a discount on everything. Stylish Pete drove stylish Mary to stylish dances at the then-stylish Hotel Syracuse.

But when the Ford broke an axle and Pete, dressed in his brothers' best clothes, had to call on those same brothers to come bail him out, Uncle Dick's response, *Well, Pete always was a good dancer,* marked my father for life as "The Good Dancer." It was code for saying that Pete was inept. Though he was a draftsman and an engineer, though he had a magic touch with people, he simply couldn't fix things.

That would never change.

That, however, didn't mean that things didn't get fixed. When dad was around, things somehow fixed themselves. Take the door, for example.

On a day that my brother and I remember as both wonderful and typical, Dad was trying to hang a door in the living room, a doomed effort from the start. Mom and Dad had scrimped to buy an air conditioner and, though our apartment was very small (to close the front door, you had to step into the bathroom), the only air conditioner they could afford could cool just one room, so a door had to be hung to separate the living room from the kitchen. Dad, always game, got out his tools and went to work, but there was just no way. He couldn't hang a door. He was a good dancer.

As Dad struggled in the living room, Mom was on the fire escape washing windows and answering the neighbors' *Hey, Mary, when you're done with your windows, come and do mine!* with *That'll be the day. Come on up. Pete's hanging a door.*

By the time Mom was finished with the windows, the tiny apartment was in its usual state—packed, wall-to-wall, with parents and kids, TV on, everybody arguing about umpires' calls, Dad setting the tone which invariably brought out the best in everybody, including the usually dour Mr. Neilsen, who wasn't a good dancer but he sure as hell could hang a door.

Mr. Neilsen's exquisite son, Johnny, one of my brother's closest friends, a childhood idol of mine, and the most-gifted athlete in the neighborhood, was scouted by the Yankees. Instead of playing minor league ball, he yielded to heavy pressure from his parents, went to college to study engineering, and had a nervous breakdown. When he was released from the hospital, he wasn't allowed to go home, so he moved in with Mom and Dad. *They never should have forced him to go to college, Billy. All he wanted to do was play ball and he was good!* The folks made him feel at home, coached him for job interviews, and cut his meat for him because he wasn't allowed to use a knife. So, who knows? Maybe in the long run there were more important things than being able to hang a door.

Dad's philosophy, and one of his legacies to me, was *All things work together unto the good,* and in Dad's world, they did.

Except...

Except for once a year when Mom's world fell apart and, as good a dancer as he was, he simply couldn't fix it.

———

### The Orchids

My mother.

*When I was a kid, Billy, just a little kid, they'd let me out of school early to start the supper. My mother gave me one match, just one, to light the oven, and if I couldn't light it with that match, well then, God help me....*

The crack in my mother's world was her rage, which I knew, even if she did not, came from the poverty of her childhood years. But my mother's rage was far too large for any one childhood. It was the rage of generations of impoverished childhoods before hers, a rage reaching back to a genocidal famine that drove the Irish from their homes. It was a rage that, in the Old World, led futile rebellions, and, in the New, built railroads, dug canals and, on occasion, tore the hell out of our apartment.

It was a rage, against all odds, to live.

That rage, harnessed for a family facing heavy odds, was monumentally helpful. *Billy, when your father and I came to New York we had but nothing. No heat, no hot water. Nothing. Your brother was four months old and his carriage was the only furniture we had. Your father and I, Billy, we didn't have two nickels to rub together.* Rage made a home for us out of but-nothing. Fed us on but-nothing. *I used to pop pennies out of lucky horseshoes to buy a can of tuna for the creamed tuna on toast* (which was good money wasted as far as I was concerned). Above all, it protected my brother and me from the humiliations my mother had felt as a child. *I remember once my mother came home from work, Billy, she washed floors for the Colemans (they were always very good to my mother, Billy, they worshiped her). She came home late—my brother and I were in bed—but she got us up and brought us downstairs to show Mrs. Coleman she wasn't lying. See, Mrs.*

*Coleman wouldn't believe that we slept in flour sacks. My
mother, Billy, she could sew anything....*

Even though Mary Cain's children might have no heat
or hot water on winter mornings, she'd be god-damned if
they'd be cold. She would get up long before us, swearing
at the slumlord who owned our apartment building, and,
with her one match, light our somewhat iffy gas stove
and put our clothes in the oven to warm them so that, by
the time we got up, we could jump right from a warm bed
into clothes that were, if anything, too hot. So my brother
and I, on but-nothing, ended up more pampered than
poor.

My mother's rage, turned outward, was a tremen-
dously creative force. But when her aim was bad and that
vast rage turned on the family...

And it was honestly hard for Mom to pick her targets well.
Circumstances confused her aim from the start. It wasn't
the fashion when she was small for a child to be angry with
a father for dying.... And how could Mary-in-the-flour-
sack (good clothes were a concern of hers till the day she
was buried) be angry with the Colemans who, though they
exploited my grandmother and humiliated my mother,
were so personally kind that, even in Mom's old age, they
were fondly remembered.

But the anger had to go somewhere, so...

When Mom's anger turned on the family...

Oh, let's say, one Easter, Aunt Marg's husband, Uncle Doc,
gave orchids to all my father's sisters, but not to my
mother who was staying with them.... And let's say Dad

found out about the flowers too late and all the stores were closed and there was nothing to be done.... And let's say Mom—with all the rage that should have been spent on famines and death—blamed him for what she felt was her humiliation and demanded that he fix the crack that had opened in her world and he couldn't because, well, *Pete always was a good dancer....* It was then that the boulder would begin to roll down the mountain, and then God help us all.

Her rage, mixed with endless grief, could shake the walls. Could shake the house. Could shake tears out of me because I wanted my wonderful father to fix what was wrong and I could not understand why he could not do it.

You see, I thought it was simple at the time.

I thought it was about orchids.

———

But the rage that could shake the house could *not* shake my father.

If he could not fix what was wrong—and he could not—he could stand in the way of the ensuing fury.

And he did.

He deeply believed in Rule #3.

The parents' problems were not the kids' business and Dad (his glasses framed in thin golden wire) would take the brunt of it. His mantra to me was *I've got broad shoulders, Billy. Don't worry about it,* but I did.

I would watch him reason with her, battle with her, accompany her where the fury took her, try to comfort her, and yet never be able to bring her peace.

———

## *My Father Leaves the Room*

It was a great shock to me when my father died.

*I don't want to die in a hospital, Mary, said my father. You won't, Pete,* Mary answered—and he didn't.

Pete died before the dark undercurrent in my parents' marriage could be resolved. It seemed to me a serious violation of Rule #1. My father had left the room before the fight was over.

It wasn't like him and I was astonished. Maybe Uncle Dick had been right and the good dancer had just danced away. I know Dad wasn't responsible for dying, but even so, I felt somehow betrayed. Perhaps all things did not work together unto the good.

————

We are not a family that goes to cemeteries. Oh, we went to Dad's grave once or twice, mostly for form's sake, but that wore out quickly. (See Rule #4: Nobody cares what the neighbors think.) A mound of grass and a stone with dad's name on it meant nothing to us and we never went again.

So, finally, it was Dad who had to come to us.

————

He came to me several times in dreams (typically enough, in sports stadiums), but with Mom, who wasn't given to symbolic dreaming, he had to be more direct.

————

Several years after Dad died, while I was visiting Syracuse, Mom mentioned, as we were unpacking groceries, apropos of buying a new car, that Dad had been by and they had discussed it. I assumed I had misunderstood, but when I asked her when he had been by, she said, *Just the other day and he thinks I should buy the car.*

*Dad? Dad...was here? Just the other day?*

*Oh, yes. Dad was here. He comes by now and then. After Sister Ann Louise was here to visit, he stayed a long time.*

My mother evidently didn't think of her dead husband's dropping by the house as at all extraordinary until I started treating it as if it were. That began to make her uncomfortable and, as she didn't want to be uncomfortable about having her Pete in the house, she tried to end the conversation. But I pressed on: *What do you mean he was here? What was it like? Was he old or young? Did you talk to him?* I really wanted to know more, but the last question *Did you talk to him?* was a mistake. It gave her an easy out. It was foolish of me to ask if they had talked. If he was there, they had talked. There were few moments in their forty-year married life when they weren't talking to each other about something. Neighbors used to come to our apartment just to listen to them talk. Mom took advantage of the obviousness of my question to take offense and end the conversation: *Did I talk with him? Of course I talked with him. Billy, he's your father!*

And that was the last I ever heard about Dad's visits. Until...

———

Some years later, on another visit, Mom and I were sitting in the living room.

I was reading; Mom was just thinking as she often did.

As a child I gave up asking what she was thinking. She could never tell me. I'm not sure that she knew. *Oh, just thinking,* she'd say.

This was a quiet summer evening. Nothing special. Then she said, out of nowhere, very simply, but with a voice of absolute objective truth:

*I was too hard on him.*

Silence.

There was no need to ask about whom she was speaking. She was talking about her Pete and she said: *I was too hard on him.*

I didn't say anything. What Mom had said wasn't said to me. It was just said. *I was too hard on him.*

Silence.

When she finally looked over to me for a response, I said, I hope equally simply, *Yes. Yes, you were.* Not an accusation, but an acknowledgement of the costly truth she had finally arrived at. And she agreed with a nod. *I was. I was too hard on him.* Then she went back to her silence because, really, what more was there to say?

*I was too hard on him.*

Six words that summarized, acknowledged, and apologized for years of rage misplaced.

And that was the end of it forever.

The fight was over.

And from that time till her own death, my mother's love for my father—and she always loved him, *Billy, you could slice bread with the crease in Pete's pants*—from that moment, her love for him never ceased to grow.

So, as it turned out, my mother had the last word in the fight, but my father never needed the last word. He needed her to be happy. To be at peace. And she was. With that, the riddle was solved, a new kind of peace descended on the house and, at the time, that made me happy, but, as I write this, I am crying because, after that night, my father didn't come around much anymore. The fight was over, finally over, and, in my family, so often it was the fights that held us together.

---

### The International Chicken Wings Festival and Other Grievances

My mother and I didn't fight when I moved in to live with her for her last year.

In fact, during my first month in Syracuse, my mother and I got along like the ideal dying parent/supportive son team. She kept thanking me for being so good to her and I kept telling her that it was my privilege.

There was so much we couldn't say to one another. (A violation of rule #5.) We were afraid and our fear made us angry, but we couldn't find a way to voice the anger.

I think what we each feared was being abandoned.

We had cause.

Mom and Dad had seen their parenting job as getting my brother and me independent enough by seventeen to go into the world and start lives of our own. They succeeded. And, as Paul and I found our lives taking us to Alaska, Boston, Ireland, Oklahoma, New York, Los Angeles, Texas and Vietnam, they rejoiced with our successes, grieved with our losses. They visited us where they could and sent care packages where they couldn't. But the independence they had bred in us was backfiring on Mom in her eighties. Though she didn't say it, it was clear she was afraid that I might disappear at any moment. And God knows I wanted to.

For my part, with Mom's weight dropping drastically, I was afraid that *she* was about to disappear—literally. It took me a few days in Syracuse to realize it, but at some point my mother had given up eating solid food. When I confronted her on it, she said, *I can't eat, Billy. Please don't make me try!*

She had a point. Radiation treatment on her throat after a previous cancer surgery had left the skin on her neck the texture of petrified wood and had seriously compromised her ability to swallow. With her unwillingness to eat and consequent loss of weight and growing weakness, it seemed to me that she was trying to just fade away, to sneak out. This was so completely uncharacteristic of her that it frightened me. I was perfectly willing to help Mom die, but I needed her there, alert, communicating and, well, like herself.

Something had to be done.

I am not a good cook, but I know if you toss a quarter pound of butter and half a bottle of wine into almost anything, people will ask for seconds. So I decided to try my technique on Mom in a modified version (given all the medication, little wine, much butter).

It worked.

We went through a lot of butter, but she ate more solids, and, as she did, she felt stronger, which surprised and delighted her.

All of which is by way of saying that, when the fight came—all families fight—it was about butter.

Or at least we thought it was about butter.

———

The fight could have come at any time.

There were a million petty annoyances that could have sparked it. I didn't know exactly what Mom's were, but all of mine could be summed up in one word: Syracuse.

———

I was born in New York City. I grew up a city kid. Always have been. Always will be. The joy most people derive from sunsets I get from looking at the Williamsburg Bridge. I thrive on the atmosphere, pace, and culture of New York City, so when I asked Cathy, Mom's cleaning-lady-and-psychotherapist, if there were any cultural events to look forward to in Syracuse, and she informed me, without irony, that there was an International Chicken Wings Festival coming up at the mall, I suddenly felt very trapped, very resentful.

We could have fought then.

But we didn't.

———

Still, in moving to Syracuse, I thought that since I am a writer (as a priest I have taught, done retreat work, etc., but currently, I write), I could keep some version of my own life going as long as I had my computer and a little electricity.

The electricity went out for the first time on November 1st.

The lights flickered and, as my writing disappeared before my eyes, my laptop began to beep, letting me know the battery wasn't charged. Syracuse, notorious for its brutal winters, was having "an early dusting" of wet, heavy snow knocking out power all over the city.

Now, if I had any sense, any sense at all, I would have gone outside and made a snowman with the kids who had the day off from school, but I didn't. I chose to brood. I made a cup of coffee with tepid tap water and brooded.

We could have had a fight then—but we didn't.

———————

Since I was not especially interested in the International Chicken Wings Festival, I spent a lot of time in the evening watching TV with Mom. This was a mistake.

My mother can click past five Academy Award movies, and if she can't find the Knicks or the Mets, say *Nothing on*, click to CNN for the night and refuse to yield the remote.

When I tried to introduce her to PBS, she had an odd reaction. The shows pretty much bored her, but she watched the fundraising sequences with remarkable intensity. When I asked her what caught her interest she said, *Well, I know it's a telethon, but I can't figure out what the disease is*. So much for PBS.

So we would usually end up clicking back and forth between both of our shows. On a good night, we would get just enough of each show to be frustrated with not seeing it all; on a bad night, we caught every commercial on both stations.

We could have fought about TV. But we didn't.

Which brings us to the butter.

———————

### NOVEMBER 16
### *Butter*

Carol, the home-health-aide-who-buys-Mom-cigarettes, called up and offered to do some shopping for us on her way over.

I was grateful. If Carol could pick up a few essentials, she'd save me a trip to the store later, and I could get some writing done.

As I was talking to Carol, Mom, as she often does when I'm on the phone (and this drives me crazy), began a parallel conversation with me. (Have I said this drives me crazy?) She wanted to know who was on the phone and what was going on. I told her Carol was offering to stop at Byrne Dairy on the way over and wanted to know what we needed. *Oh! How nice! Make sure you thank her.*

So far, so good. I thanked Carol and told her we needed milk and butter. Then Mom said, *No BUTTER!* and we were off.

I said (covering the phone), *Don't worry, Mom, I'll take care of this,* and told Carol, *Milk and butter.*

Mom then said, louder this time, with the conviction of Luther saying "Here I stand" or MacArthur promising to return: *No BUTTER!*

Carol said, *What was that?* and I said, *Milk and . . .* and she said, *No, I mean in the background.*

And I said, *Don't worry about that,* and Mom said again—louder—*NO BUTTER.*

Carol, a mother herself and therefore of the same union as Mom, said, *But what's your MOTHER saying?*

I said, *Carol, please, it will save me some time this afternoon if you'll pick up some milk and . . .*

Mom, now sounding like a political prisoner trying to get a message out of jail, said, *CAROL, NO BUTTER! NO BUTTER, CAROL!* Then, to me, *TELL HER I SAID NO BUTTER!*

And I, unable to handle the two conversations at the same time, said (coolly and rationally, I thought), *CAROL, BUY THE BUTTER! BUY MILK AND BUTTER!* Then I hung up the phone, turned to Mom, and said, *Now what was THAT all about,* and the fight was on.

I was told emphatically that *Carol buys only THE MILK,* and I said, *Well that may very well BE, but TODAY she's buying the milk AND THE BUTTER and what the hell was wrong with THAT?* and was told that Mom *HATES BYRNE DAIRY BUTTER.* She wants *LAND O' LAKES LIGHTLY SALTED BUTTER,* which they *DON'T SELL* at *BYRNE DAIRY.* And I said that Carol getting the *BYRNE DAIRY BUTTER* would save *ME* a trip to the store so that I could (escalating) *MAYBE get some WORK done FOR A CHANGE,* and she said (escalating), *WORK! WORK! WORK! That's ALL you ever THINK about,* and I said (escalating), *Now I WONDER where I got THAT from* and *if that WAS all I ever THOUGHT about I'd be in* (escalating) *NEW YORK* right now and *NOT* in (escalating) *GOD–DAMNED SYRACUSE,* home of the *GOD-DAMNED INTERNATIONAL CHICKEN WINGS FESTIVAL* at the *GOD-DAMNED MALL,* and she said (escalating), *DON'T YOU SWEAR IN MY HOUSE,* and she *HATED* having to *ASK* me to be in *SYRACUSE* but there wasn't a *GOD-DAMNED THING* she could *DO* about it since (final escalation) —

*SHE DIDN'T WANT TO GET THE CANCER IN THE FIRST PLACE! AND BESIDES, NOW THAT I WAS HERE SHE COULDN'T EVEN WATCH HER OWN SHOWS IN HER OWN HOUSE ANY MORE!* and I told her that *I WAS SORRY SHE HAD CANCER, VERY, VERY SORRY! BUT—IT WASN'T MY FAULT,* and continuing in this coolly rational vein, I explained to her that her shows were *MORONIC* and that I was doing the best I could for her but half the time *SHE WOULDN'T EVEN EAT AND HOW THE HELL WAS I SUPPOSED TO HELP HER IF SHE WOULDN'T EVEN EAT FOR CHRIST'S SAKE,* and she said *I TOLD YOU NOT TO SWEAR! AND THE RADIATION TREATMENTS HAD TAKEN AWAY HER SENSE OF TASTE! AND—*

*IT WAS* HARD *TO EAT IF YOU COULDN'T EVEN* TASTE THE FOOD!!!

And I said—

*WELL,*
*IF*
*YOU*
*CAN'T*
*EVEN*
TASTE *IT—*
*WHAT THE HELL DIFFERENCE*
*DID IT MAKE IF IT WAS*
BYRNE DAIRY BUTTER
*OR* LAND O'LAKES LIGHTLY SALTED!?!

At which point Carol arrived with the butter.

———

Carol knew immediately something was wrong and, as she sat down to take off her boots (more snow, constant snow, record-setting snow that winter) she wanted to know what was up.

So we told her.

We started from the top and had the whole fight, pretty much verbatim, all over again.

Carol, who had been exposed mostly to our dying mother/ideal son mode, was pretty much slack-jawed at this display, after which she said, sensibly, *Well, if you had told me, I could have stopped at another store and gotten you the Land o' Lakes Lightly Salted.*

Carol's solution to the problem was so simple, so elegant, so easy, that my mother and I looked at each other, smiled foolishly, and then, we laughed. Really laughed. Laughed like we hadn't laughed since this whole ordeal began.

Carol, a good scout, laughed along with us, but when she wanted to know what we were all laughing about, we couldn't really tell her.

Part of it, of course, was sheer relief. All the anger that had been lurking around was finally out where we could see it and there was nothing in it that we couldn't handle. I suppose we were both madder at the cancer than we were at anything else....

But relief alone didn't quite explain the distinct note of joy in our laughter...and the joy came from the fight itself. As long as we were fighting, the old rules were back in play and that meant our worst fears about each other would not be realized. No matter what happened, as long as either of us could help it—

Nobody was going to leave that room.

### *Chapter 4. The Six Commandments*

Every family has its own rules—covenants—to hold the family together.

Even the Ten Commandments—which we look on as a guide to personal morality—were a way of holding the family together.

I have formulated the rules in my family retroactively. We certainly never laid them out on tablets of stone. But they were understood and, by and large, they were followed.

What were the rules—spoken and unspoken—in your family? What were the covenants that joined you together? Protected you from harm? And what—if any—were the rules that were harmful?

Jesus was able to summarize the law and the prophets in two rules: love of God and love of neighbor as one's self.

What, I wonder, in your family, is the hardest of those commandments—love of God, neighbor, or self?

# 5

# *Thanksgiving*

---

*Bill, the Boston College–Notre Dame game is on. Kick-off in five minutes.*

It's the BC/Notre Dame game today, but another day it could just as easily be *Billy, the president's going to be on. Press conference in five minutes.* Or *Jury's in. Verdict coming up.* Mom has CNN, Headline News, C-Span, the Weather Channel, two ESPNs, and Court TV and she loves them all. *Big storm coming, Billy. The airports are going to be a madhouse. Come see.* Thanks to cable, my mother—housebound except for trips to Dr. P and Gloria the hairdresser—my mother stays better informed than most presidents. *Oh, Billy, come and see!*

Responding to the urgency of her announcements, I usually put my work on hold and join her. Given the number of press conferences, briefings, verdicts, photo opportunities, and natural disasters broadcast daily, we keep pretty busy.

*Oh, Billy, come on out and watch it with me. Boston College is up 3-0!*

And my mother, well, she's not a detached observer of events. She cares about everything she watches.

After Mom died, I asked Paulette why they had become such good friends and she said,

*Well, your mother cared, didn't she? Didn't she? I mean she really cared. About other people. People she didn't even know. I remember I told her about my nephew, poor thing, who lost his job. Mary said she'd make a novena for him. She didn't even know the boy, but she cared. He got a job too! How can you not care about somebody like that? Really? How?*

Paulette, as always, was right. Mom's caring was contagious. And that's why I had absolutely no intention of watching the BC/Notre Dame game with her.

*It's 10-nothing, Bill! Boston's going to win it! You have to see this!*

Mom would say caring was a privilege, but it is also an emotional burden and, what with looking after her, working on my writing and trying to stay sane in Syracuse, I had plenty to care about without adding a football team to the mix.

*Oh my God, Billy. 10-7! Notre Dame's coming back. Come on out!*

Although I got my undergraduate degree from BC, I was there for only two years. By the time I got to the Heights, I had, in a cascading series of majors, attended several other colleges, so I wasn't really there long enough to develop any school loyalty. My parents did, though. They fell in love with the place the first weekend they saw it. In fact, Dad asked me to loan him a large textbook to carry around so he could feel like he fit in. And, as always, their loyalties were deep....

*Oh my God, Billy, BC-12; Notre Dame-7! Billy, you've got to come out and watch this. I'm near losing my mind!*

Besides, BC was the underdog in this game, and I didn't feel that I needed another underdog at this particular point in my life. So I went back to my work, the writing project whose deadline was becoming frighteningly imminent.

———

By the middle of the second quarter, Mom wasn't only announcing touchdowns, she was knocking on my door to announce every play.

As it became clear that no further writing was going to be done, I joined her, resolving beforehand not to waste any emotional energy that could be used later for writing. To this end, I rehearsed an old and reliable mantra: *It's just a game, it's just a game, it's just a game...*

By the time I arrived, Mom was sitting so far forward on her rocking chair that I thought it might dump her on the floor. Tense as a sprinter in the blocks, she was playing every down of the game along with the players, shouting instructions to the coaches, protesting calls, encouraging her team and laughing at herself for doing all of the above.

I could relax and enjoy this because, after all, it was just a game.

Besides, there was no need to worry.

By the fourth quarter, BC had rolled up a seemingly invincible 31-17 lead.

Then the BC quarterback fumbled a snap—*Oh, Nooooo* —setting up a Notre Dame touchdown and point after.

38-25!

It's just a game.

Then *Oh my GOD! NO!*

Another bobbled snap and another Notre Dame touchdown.

38-32!

Just a game. A game. A . . .

*Oh, God! Oh, Billy, they can't lose it now!!!*

But they could.

My mother shuts her eyes tight. I know her well enough to know that she's not wincing or distancing herself. She's praying. Or, at least, what my mother would call prayer. My mother is petitioning an infinite God for a finite goal. A field goal, in point of fact. Does God care about the outcome of the BC-Notre Dame game? Maybe not. On the other hand, maybe . . .

BC is forced to punt, and, with 1:09 remaining, Notre Dame takes the lead for the first time in the game, 39-38. "Cheer, Cheer for Old Notre Dame" rings out.

My mother, however, will concede nothing.

There's a minute-nine left and, while there's a minute nine left, my mother is going to care. *A field goal will do it! They can DO it!*

Maybe, but they weren't making it easy.

Incomplete pass.

*NOOOO!*

Incomplete pass/near interception.

*NOOOOOOOO!*

Third and 10, 47 seconds left.

Then, first down on BC 37!

My mother screams *GO!*

27 seconds. Pass to BC's 43.

18 seconds. Pass to Notre Dame's 33!

12 seconds.

The ball thrown away.

5 seconds.

To the ND 24 with good field position.

*I TOLD you they could do it!*

Yes, but they haven't done it yet.

This field goal—if they make it—will be a 41-yard attempt and the longest kick this kicker has ever made is 39 yards.

It doesn't look good.

*He can do it! I know he can do it! I know he can. I know he can. I know he can.*

My brother and I both feel our lives were ruined by the book *The Little Engine That Could*. Mary Cain believed there wasn't anything you couldn't do if you put your mind to it and had God on your side.

I ask how she knows he can do it.

*He's a good kid, Billy.*

How can she know that? I ask.

She says *Well, just look at him.*

So I look at him more carefully.

————

The first thing I notice is, as always with kickers, how much smaller he is than everybody else on the field.

That doesn't seem fair, given the fact that the whole game rests on him now.

And he looks so intense, so completely focused. Well, I suppose he has to be. To win the game he has to come up with a personal best.

A personal best.

In this very public spectacle, it is a very *personal* thing this guy has to do. He has to reach within himself and do what he's been doing the best he can for years, and, in front of all these people, he has to do it better.

And the majority of people in the stadium want him to fail.

That doesn't seem right.

Don't they realize that his children will know about this

moment? And his grandchildren? And millions more people all across the country are watching this decisive moment in his life. And I now deeply resent having noticed this kicker because, once you've noticed him, you can't help but care about him, and caring, once started, is almost impossible to contain. Care once started knows no boundaries. It bubbles up and washes out and over all comers.

He has to make this kick.

He *has* to.

And now that I am worried for David Gordon, kicker, I find myself worried for all other lonely people in the world on whom so much depends.

Crossing guards.

Single parents.

911 operators.

First-time surgeons.

And people who are smaller than the rest of us. Low birth-weight babies. Families that are a little short at the end of the month.

The floodgates open now and a tide of caring rushes in.

Because it's not a game.

It's not a game to David Gordon, kicker.

Finally, it's never just a game.

Every moment, every action counts, and everything and everybody in the whole world depends on everything and everybody else and absolutely everything depends on this one kick.

This kick, in fact, is the turning point of Western Civilization.

So go on, David. Go on. Don't be afraid. You *are* a good kid. You're a *good* kid and I *know* you can do it. I know you can. Down. Set. Snap.…

Suddenly every motion has the slow, tortuous clarity of a car wreck.

The snap is high! *HIGH, DAMN IT!*
*NO, IT'S OK!*
Ball placed.
The kick.
STRONG!
YES!
But—wide?
WIDE!!!
*SHIT!!!!!!!!*
NO! NOT WIDE!
IT'S—
IT'S CURVING BACK!!!
IT'S...good?
*IT'S GOOD!*
TWO POINTS! TWO POINTS! TWO POINTS!
41-39!
BC WINS! BC WINS! BC WINS!
I find myself standing and cheering.

As I turn to congratulate Mom, she has already leapt out of the chair and onto her feet.

She hurls both her arms straight over her head—which, given her physical limitations is impossible—and, with her head thrown back, a huge smile on her face, and tears in her eyes, she—dying of cancer—says in ecstasy to God and the world, *Thank you!*

———

Mom shuffled down the corridor more slowly than usual that night to say *'night, Billy.*

*Good night, Mom. Sleep well.*

*Oh, I will. I'll sleep good tonight. God, I'm SO tired.*

And I thought, *Well, why shouldn't you be? You're eighty-*

*one years old, you're dying of cancer, you played Notre Dame today.... And you won!*

———

That Thursday Mom asked if, given the trouble she has swallowing, she could celebrate Thanksgiving by *not* eating.

So our celebration was muted.

A nice grace, then Mom sipped a milkshake and I had some pasta.

There was, of course, a lot of football on TV, but since Mom was still pretty tired from having beaten Notre Dame, we watched the parade instead.

### Chapter 5. Thanksgiving

Once when I had misplaced my keys, I asked my mother for help finding them. She said, "Have you prayed to St. Anthony?" I said, "That's superstition." She said, "Find your own keys."

Yes, we give names to our religions. Catholic. Protestant. Jewish. Buddhist. And on and on. These are categories so vast they can encompass a tribe, a people, a nation.

I am one of a billion Catholics in the world and I am sure the billion of us can agree in general principles on what it means to be Catholic, but each one of us, I am sure, has some private devotion that makes their religion unique.

A football game on Thanksgiving can become a religious event.

A simple visit between cousins can become a visitation.

A birth becomes an incarnation.

A meal becomes a eucharist.

My mother eventually said her prayer (St. Anthony, please come 'round; something's lost that has to be found) and, of course, put her hand directly on the keys.

What has found the keys in your life—in your family?

What field goal has inspired infinite gratitude?

# 6

# *The Problem of Pain*

---

The doctor said Mom's dignity and comfort should be the main concern, but it never was. Not to the doctors.

If it had been, they would have done something about the pain.

Pain is the heart and the soul of it. It's the pain that causes the fear. It's the fear that causes the isolation and, finally, it's the isolation, the loneliness, that's unbearable.

Pain demands respect, and doctors, at least the doctors I dealt with, did not respect pain.

It was searching for the cause of a relentless back pain that caused the doctors to find the cancer—by mistake—in the first place. Dr. P first treated the pain with an over-the-counter medication and, when that offered no relief, he wrote a prescription for a low dosage of Darvocet. Although this failed to get my mother an undisturbed night's sleep, she could now at least walk, and the ability to move across a room became a thing of pride to her, something to show off to her friends and neighbors.

As this medication too began to fail, Dr. P was reluctant to increase the dosage. *I don't know, Mary. I could add a pill, but this might go on for a long time and we don't want to wear the medication out.* At the time, we went with Dr. P's *We can discuss it at the next visit,* not realizing that this attitude on our part would eventually reduce us to beggars.

Please help us. Please, please do something about the pain.

———

It should be said that my mother had a very high tolerance for pain.

Her constant concern for all that was going on around her, her inability to let pain be her sole concern, helped a great deal.

In one of the most astonishing moments of this whole ordeal, I came out of the back room where I had been working and found my mother completely doubled over, moaning in pain. She had one hand on her back and the other holding on to a chair for balance.

It was clear that she was in agony. I ran to her, shouting over the basketball game on television, *What's wrong? Mom, what's wrong?*

And my mother—bent double—shouted back, *Oh my God, Billy, I'm in awful pain and the Knicks are down by three!*

———

As my first month in Syracuse wore on, the medication wore out.

I tried to convince Mom to cheat on doctor's orders, but "doctor's orders" were sacred to her. The pill was to last four hours so, by God, she would make it last four hours.

But the pill did not last four hours. The pill was failing by fifteen minutes. (She would note all of this down carefully for the next doctor's visit.) So she would wait the fifteen minutes, in pain, for the next pill, but the new pill would take another fifteen minutes to work, so that, every four hours, there was an absolutely certain half-hour of intense pain, and that half-hour became a thing to dread. Before long we were utterly preoccupied by time, and not in the right way. The question should have been *How can I enjoy the precious hours I have left?* but it became *Oh, God, how can I possibly make it through the next half hour?*

The only thing that seemed to distract Mom effectively was televised ice skating. Mom had been a champion ice skater as a kid. I found the medals in the closet.

Fortunately, since the Winter Olympics were coming up, there was a lot of skating on. Paulette and Mom's other friends would call up, shout, telegram-like, *Ice skating on channel 24,* and hang up. We would flick to 24 immediately and watch endless toe loops, Salchows, Hamill camels, and inside death spirals. *I don't care if they do fall down, Billy. I think they're great. All of them.*

And so we watched them—all of them—endlessly.

And it helped.

As the guaranteed half-hour of pain lengthened into an hour, I began to feel that we were dealing with an inside death spiral of our own. I did what I could by trying to talk her through it, but that was pretty much useless.

You can't talk pain away; you can't give it away; you can't even share it. The best I could do was to keep her company.

We would walk. Stand. Sit. Change positions again and again, each position seeming to give comfort for a minute. Two minutes. Change positions again. *Just let me lie down for a minute, Billy. Maybe I can sleep.* Then, a minute later, *Oh my God, Billy, help me up.* And always, *How much longer do we have to go?* Occasionally I would come back from the store and find Mom absolutely wild, quite literally pounding on the walls. That was bad, very bad, but it was not the worst.

At the worst, there was no activity at all.

Mom would curl up in a little ball on the couch, her face all pulled tight to the center in wicked concentration, and this woman who was interested in absolutely everything became interested in absolutely nothing. Nothing but pain. All she could think about, feel about, talk about... was pain.

———

At the start I respected her concern about the prescribed interval between pills.

Sometimes, I began to shave time off. Sometimes, it was too late. The pain had gotten ahead of us and another day was shot to hell. One of my few regrets about the entire time of my mother's dying is that I didn't say *to hell with it* a lot more often.

I don't know what we could have said to have educated Dr. P to what we were going through. What should we have said that we did not say? We did educate him eventually, but that wasn't until July and this was only December.

———

*DECEMBER 2*

We see the doctor.

Pain is the only agenda as far as I am concerned. Mom and I carefully describe what we have been going through; all Mom's careful notes are decoded and shared, all my compromises exposed. Dr. P nods as if he understands and, after some conversation, he says, *Mary, there's no reason for you to ever be in pain.* Mom's fearful face relaxes on hearing this. He ups the dosage a pill a day and adds another pill at bedtime. Good news. Mom and I exchange a relieved look as he writes the prescription. Then, as he hands us the prescription he says: *Mary, you could have years ahead of you and you can wear out the dosage to the point where you can be taking a pill a minute. So I have to warn you. I won't increase the pain medication after this....*

And with that warning, the fear returns.

———

We never did find out what was actually causing the pain. We never knew if it was the result of old surgeries, osteoporosis, or as the doctor once hinted, cancer in the marrow of the bone. But, by the time Mom died, eight months later, I felt that I did know the cause of the pain.

In the end, it was the doctor who caused the pain by refusing to alleviate it.

### Chapter 6. The Problem of Pain

I have never suffered severe pain, so I don't want to provide any easy answers.

Eventually we came up with a treatment for the pain, but until we did, it caused terrible fear in us.

A sense of dread that attacked our hope.

How we deal with the pain tells us a great deal about understanding and compassion—but no, I don't want to wander into clichés, not about pain.

I know this much.

It is hard to be with a person in pain.

But it's even harder if you avoid the connection that might break the isolation of pain and give companionship.

Perhaps you know more about this mystery than I do.

If you do, you have my sympathy and my respect.

Teach me what you have learned.

# 7

# The Dead Sea Closets

In New York, when I need a break from writing, I browse my way through one of my neighborhood's many bookstores.

I avoid the well-organized superstores and head for the dark, cramped aisles of the used book shops where unwanted books are recycled by surly, very well-informed clerks. Browsing in the accepted and accepting chaos of the used book store is exactly what I need when I hit a roadblock in my own writing. I never know what I'm looking for, but I think there is always a vague hope in the back of my mind that the late James Agee might have written a new book. It's a long shot, but as good an excuse as any to explore. And without really looking for anything at all, I occasionally find what I've been looking for all the time. Once I came across a leather-bound, mint condition 1900 edition of Shakespeare's Complete Works, illustrated with photographs of the Irving/Terry productions of the plays. I couldn't believe how perfect it was. I knew I couldn't afford it, so I put it back without checking the price. Then, as I was leaving, I checked the price. $4. I walked out with a treasure and went back to my writing.

There are few used bookstores here in Syracuse, New York. None nearby. Besides, the winter is so punishing that it's hard enough just to get out to buy food. When I do make it to the mall bookstore, the offerings are pretty much limited to the latest mysteries, romances, and movie novelizations. At the start, I did have hopes.

When I first went to the brightly lit store at the mall and asked for Shakespeare, the cheerful clerk thought for a moment and then said, *Shakespeare? We don't have his plays, but I think we have some of his novels.*

*Shakespeare's novels?* I asked. *Really? Shakespeare's novels?* And she said, *Oh, yes, I'm quite sure we have at least some of his novels here.* And I thought, Well, this might be a better bookstore than I thought. It wasn't. What they had was *Lamb's Tales from Shakespeare.* When the clerk saw I was disappointed, she offered to order Shakespeare's novels for me, if I didn't mind the wait.

———

So, no bookstores to browse and snowed in half the time.

As an alternative to climbing the walls, I have begun to browse the apartment's closets. Browse is the wrong word. The sheer density of our closets, which have never been cleaned, *I'll get around to it someday, Billy. I won't die before I do the closets—I promise you that,* precludes anything as casual as browsing. You don't browse my family's closets; you excavate. Over the years, my parents, by putting anything-not-immediately-needed but still too-valuable-to-be-thrown-away in the closets, have created, stratum by stratum, a multi-chambered time capsule reaching back a century.

I know it isn't exactly a dig in the Sinai. I know the closets aren't the Dead Sea caves that protected documents from the biblical era until they were uncovered by children playing. But what a find. So I dig. Who knows what might turn up? A lost gospel? I have found unexpected treasure before.

———

The search begins with a struggle through the most recent past, mostly boxes of medical bills, paid or referred to insurance companies.

*Don't throw them away, Billy. You never know.* This layer is interesting only ecologically. To keep this constant THIS IS NOT A BILL correspondence going, whole forests in Oregon have been turned into pulp. Sad, but onward through the protective sediment of dusty garment bags, skeins of yarn from abandoned knitting project—*I just don't have the energy*—and old gag Christmas presents. Dig past the Cretaceous level quickly. The artifacts of my brother's and my adult lives are still too familiar to be of any serious interest. On to the Jurassic period.

The Jurassic period!

The age when Children Freely Roamed the Earth. Vast material here. Birth certificates with tiny inky footprints on paper. Vaccination forms. Photographs. Endless photographs. Endless faces of children and young parents. Snowmen. Birthday cakes. The giant balloons from the Macy's parade. Central Park in every season. Enough pictures of us kids in every corner of New York for future archaeologists to reconstruct the city, if the need should ever arise.

And my first real find.

My mother's handwritten list of my brother's "firsts," including the date on which my brother first spit up creamed broccoli. Why did she write that down? Have to ask her.

This is a good box. Dig in this box.

———

At first Mom had me convinced that she was annoyed with my digging. She'd say, *Now why are you bringing all this stuff out here, cluttering everything up?*

Each of us has a private time of day. My mother is up long before me, and I am up long after her. All serious archaeology takes place on the night shift, and I leave my finds on the kitchen table for the day shift to discover. My first clue that she enjoyed what I was leaving out came when I would try to put any of the clutter away. She'd say *Not yet.* And I noticed too that, while Mom would complain to Paulette, *He's getting into everything,* she would also speak—briefly, but with warmth—about whatever I had left out the night before.

So, I kept on.

———

On to the Triassic.

My parent's young adulthood.

Another find here.

A black leather case that sits heavily in my hands. Inside —I remember—are Dad's drafting tools. As I hold the case, a sense of presence fills the room. It is this sense of presence that is the soul of all archaeology, from work on these closets to discoveries in the Valley of the Kings. The past reawakened in the present.

Quietly, I open the case.

My father's hands held these weighty metal compasses and templates, and I find them here, exactly as his hands have left them, each tool resting snugly within its own perfectly shaped indentation in the dark blue velvet that lines the box. When we were kids, these were our favorite forbidden toys. Now, in an age of computer-generated graphics, they look as antique as an astrolabe. And as beautiful. Perhaps I'll polish them and send them to my brother for Christmas. I think he would love them. Before putting this case aside, I find myself kissing it gently. Do real archaeologists do this with their treasures? I bet they do, and I bet they won't admit it.

Onward...

———

The Paleozoic layer and here I find the only professional photograph ever taken of my mother—a beautiful young woman in her early twenties.

Well, she did have another picture of herself taken more recently, but I don't think it counts. In her late seventies, Mom went to the mall at Christmas time and had her picture taken sitting on the knee of a depart-ment store Santa. *He was a lovely boy from Liverpool, Billy. He's getting married in the spring.* She wanted the picture to outdo the picture my brother and I had taken with an equally young Santa the previous year. But the Santa picture reassuringly captures my mother's spirit; the professional picture does not. It's so unlike my

mother that it's disorienting. More on that later. Put this picture aside and onward to the next layer.

————

Mom's school days.

Official looking documents tied with faded red bows. Diplomas? Too many of them. Not diplomas. What then? Perfect Attendance Certificates for every year she attended the Andrew Burr Blodgett Vocational School. Perfect attendance? *Every* year?

I find myself getting angry.

As my brother and I were growing up, an exaggerated sense of personal responsibility was drilled into us. Neither of us has ever been able to shake it even though it has made—and continues to make—impossible demands on us. If my mother had had the common decency to miss one day of school a year (or at least one day one year), if she had given in to human weakness (called in sick, cut a day!) our lives might have been much, much easier. But no, perfect god-damned attendance. Toss these certificates back in the box? Burn them? No, what the hell, leave them out on the kitchen table for her to gloat over. Onward...

————

I am the child of older parents who were themselves the children of older parents, so I never knew any of my grandparents. And there were never any pictures of them displayed. Even so, I immediately recognize my mother's father in a picture found at the bottom of a box in the back of the closet. She looks exactly like him. It's her as a young man. He is the proprietor of a stately turn-of-the-century bar, serving a stein of beer to a man who looks like W. C. Fields, only more so. I find other pictures of him as well. The only candid shot is a lovely picture of him and Johanna his wife on a farm, holding a beautiful dog. My grandparents— young. Close. Enjoying one another. Put these aside. Put them aside carefully. Put everything aside at this level. It is all that is left of them. Sadly, it's not much. In fact, after much looking, I find only three things that speak of what they were like as people.

The first I find among the most serious documents. Preserved among the birth certificates, citizenship papers and deeds to cemetery lots, is a handwritten recipe:

**Two gallons of rum punch**
*3 syphons selzer 2 qts. rhine wine 2 qts. brandy*
*1 qt. sherry wine 1 qt. rum*
*2 oz. pineapple extract*
*4 oz. maraschino.*
*Sweeten to taste.*

I find myself wondering what they thought two ounces of pineapple extract was going to do in all that liquor? Still, it's a good find. Not the Dead Sea Scrolls, but a good find nonetheless. The second find, even better.

Pages and pages of songs and poems. All handwritten. All in pencil. Written in Ireland and then sent to America with Broady Ryan Garrick, who is gone to America,

*To William Dawson*
*423 Schuyler St. Syracuse*
*NY US America*

My grandmother was a Ryan, so Broady must have been her sister. Thank you for the songs, Broady. And then—

Two letters.

Out of all the correspondence of a lifetime, only two letters are saved. And they are about the family dog—the dog in the picture I found.

Evidently, when my grandparents moved from the country life of Weedsport to the urban life of Syracuse, reluctant to subject the dog to city life, they put an ad in the paper trying to get him a good rural home. The only two letters that have been saved from their entire lives are the responses of the two petitioners to that ad. Strange. Still, I have no question as to who got the dog.

### Response 1:

Saw your ad in Syracuse Herald abt. dog. what do you ask for him. If you dont want a fancy price, can use him.

Yours — John W. Haywood

### and Response 2:

About your dog. He can live out his natural life with us.

You can ask Dr. Ball at Frank Mattys about us he comes to the farm once a year.

We want the dog for a barn dog there is a large up to date barn and a good deal of grain we are building a 10 room house and hope to have it completed by Dec —

You are welcome to come to the farm and see our buildings and your dog at any time.

Be sure to give us his name and will it be necessary to tie him for a few days? I do not believe in tying a dog it was not necessary with either of the ones we have.

Yours Very Truly D. D. Donelly

After thanking God for the D. D. Donellys of this world, I find that I want to know more about my grandparents. I want to drink rum punch with them while listening to them sing their songs and recite their poems with the dog sleeping in the corner.

Absurdly, I find I really want to know the dog's name.

Onward, ever more carefully...

———

Moving toward the limits of human memory now, and a bit beyond. The Precambrian level. What's here?

One picture. Mounted on a hard board, a picture of a gathering of several generations of my hard, ancient, unsmiling relatives.

(A question: Exactly when did it become compulsory to smile in photographs? From the beginning of time until relatively recently, people—including my relatives here—presented themselves for posterity seriously. Was there some event in the first half of the twentieth century so remarkably cheerful that everyone, from that time forward, has had to smile as their picture is taken? A serious archaeological question, but beyond my field of study here.)

These unsmiling folks are clearly family members on Mom's side, but, like the dog, they too have somehow become detached from their names. It seems so unfair. Why in the world should I know the names of the men who wanted my grandparents' dog and not know which one of the people in this picture is my great-grandfather? Why didn't somebody write down who was who? Weren't they thinking of me at all? Who can I ask? There is so much I want to ask....

Please, sir, which one of you terribly serious-looking people invented the rum punch? And who of you sent to

Ireland for the handwritten songs? And who sang them?
And would you mind singing them just once more so I
could hear how they went and the sound of your voice
singing them?

Silence.

And even in the silence, I enjoy their company. And find
it touching that, although they're all dead and gone, in the
pictures, some of them are still so young.

―――――

In the mornings, I ask Mom what she remembers.

Hoping to save some of these memories, I have bought
a small tape recorder to preserve her stories. Bad idea and I
should have known. Mom, unlike Dad, doesn't turn the
past into stories. She turns it into silence. Into stillness. Into
*Oh, just thinking.* So all posterity is going to get on tape from
my mother are multiple variations of *Billy, turn that damn
thing off.*

―――――

Of all the pieces of the past, the one that draws her into the
most complete stillness, into the deepest silence, is that professional photograph of her.

So, let's consider it.

It was taken for publicity purposes for the *President's
Birthday Ball* in honor of FDR. This was an enormous, talk-
of-the-town, fundraising event for the March of Dimes,
and Mom was one of the chief organizers. *We took over all
the hotels in downtown. Raised a lot of money. It was quite an
event, Billy.* And they spared no expense, it seems, for this
ten-by-fourteen-inch photograph is in a *Portrait by Bachrach*
folder.

The picture itself.

A young woman in her early twenties.

Her pitch-black hair is pulled back, but not tightly. *It was always curly. Everybody always loved it.* Lipstick and light makeup. She is wearing what looks to me like an expensive blouse. Silk. Black. Very dramatic. Closed at the neck with a jeweled, bow-shaped brooch. Against the black blouse, dramatic.

Her expression?

I would say that this young woman is serene.

Ready for what may come, but not preoccupied by it. She assumes, I think, that whatever may come will be good.

It is a lovely picture.

But, in spite of the fact that this young woman is recognizably my mother, it is a picture of a person I do not know. She is as strange to me as the unnamed relatives from our most distant past.

And this is what I find disorienting.

This serene young woman gives me the sense that, for all that I know about my mother, and, at this point I know her better than any other person in the world, all my knowledge is, finally, superficial.

Who is this girl?

Well, she is not my mother.

Lipstick? A jeweled brooch? Expensive clothes?

Never.

My mother never wore makeup. Or jewelry. And she was utterly incapable of buying herself anything unless it had been repeatedly marked down. *It used to make your father angry,* she'd say. *He'd always tell me, "Mary, if you like it, buy it. For Christ's sake, it's not a house and a lot." But I never could. I could just never spend the money. . . .*

But more than these superficial differences, the girl in this picture is missing all the qualities that make my mother my mother. The strength. The wit. The readiness to come back at you. To give as good as she got. The arched eyebrow that says *What are you up to now?*

All that hard wisdom—all that is completely missing.

This picture was taken before she developed any of her strengths.

Before she needed them.

But who... who could she have possibly been before all of that?

Who is this girl?

On first seeing this picture, Mom dismissed it with a wisecrack.

*I was Miss Big Shot, wasn't I?*

But when everything else gets put back into the closet, this picture stays out on the table. And not the kitchen table. The table in the living room.

*Not yet,* she says. *Not yet.*

I catch her looking at it on occasion. More than looking at it. Drawing strength from it. Like an icon.

And it is a bit icon-like. For one thing, there's the sky-ey photographer's studio background, the look off into the distance, and the peaceful solitude of the girl.

And even that's odd.

Solitude?

Mom? Alone?

No Pete.

No kids.

No friends.

The frame is all hers for the moment. It's just her. And she looks perfectly content with that.

And she, who cannot bear to look at pictures of herself now, *Take them away, Billy. Aren't they terrible? Terrible!* She cannot stop looking at this picture.

Who is this girl?

She is certainly not the woman who makes Mom wince when she catches sight of her in the mirror now. This picture is so distinct from that woman that it might as well be a different person altogether. Possibly a relative—a daughter or a granddaughter perhaps—but still a completely different person from Mary Cain.

And this difference is good.

Very good.

This is a difference to be cherished.

It is this complete difference that lets her pour out such unreserved affection on this girl in the black blouse. All the love she has routinely bestowed on other people, but has never been able to extend to herself—all this she can offer the girl in the picture.

She'd buy this girl expensive clothes.

I know she would. In a second, she would.

And not a drop, not an instant, not a crystal of this love is wasted, for the girl it is lavished on is closer to her than any daughter or granddaughter could ever be.

Who is this girl?

It is her.

Before cancer, before age.

Before wisdom, before strength.

Before husband, before children.

It is her.

And her alone.

And when she is lost in this picture, it is her very self that she is enjoying so deeply, offering such respect, loving so freely.

It is her.

And this is the law and the prophets.

This is what Jesus meant when he said to love one another as yourself. That's what she's doing right now, tonight, looking at that picture.

And when she does this, she stands with God on the sixth day of creation, as he sees the man, and, more to the point, the woman he has made new that day. Seeing with a clear and objective eye, and knowing, without reservation or criticism, that she is good.

This is what my mother achieves unselfconsciously as she looks at this young girl.

And this is what is called a state of grace.

*I was Miss Big Shot, wasn't I? Wasn't I?*

————

My third favorite line in all of scripture (after *Sarah laughed* and *Jesus wept*) is from the Sermon on the Mount.

It goes, *The light of the body is the eye; if therefore thine eye be single, thy whole body shall be full of light.* I don't have to take that on faith anymore. I can see it happening right in front of me.

This wrinkled, bent, old woman, missing teeth, with a slightly drooping lip from a nerve accidentally cut during a surgery on her throat—she looks with great love at this perfectly symmetrical, wrinkleless girl and her eye is, indeed, single.

And, slowly, bent and broken as she is, on this dark winter's night, her body fills with light.

————

Very soon, this old lady sitting at the table will be gone. And when she goes, she will take the girl in the photo with her.

How long, I wonder, before her name is lost?

And when even her name is lost, what will remain?

When the complete contents of these packed closets are

reduced to the Precambrian layer in the closet of her grand-daughter's granddaughter, what, I wonder, will remain of her?

I wonder.

A few stories?

The perfect attendance certificates?

And—whatever else—I hope, this picture.

### Chapter 7. The Dead Sea Closets

*"The best way to choose what to keep and what to throw away is to take each item in one's hand and ask: 'Does this spark joy?' If it does, keep it. If not, dispose of it. This is not only the simplest but also the most accurate yardstick by which to judge."*

— *Marie Kondo*

Dispose of anything that fails to give you joy?

If I followed this rule, I would never throw away anything —or at least not anything of the past.

So many things that are no longer of use evoke a moment, a memory, and give me delight.

The symbol of this is the most useless thing I can think of—the top of a cardboard box, the box itself having been thrown away decades ago. I find it impossible to get rid of.

My father wrote on it, in his beautiful draftsman's hand,

*Billy's Stuff. And I mean "stuff" in the best possible way.*

I can't throw away this cardboard box top with my father's writing on it. Holding it—I still feel his love, his humor, his presence.

All the "stuff" that was in the box is long gone.

The love is not.

One of my Dead Sea Scrolls.

I hope you have some things that are equally foolish so I feel less foolish about mine.

# 8

# *The Sons of Cain*

### December 25

And the Lord said unto Cain, *Where is Abel, thy brother?*
And he said, *I know not. Am I my brother's keeper?*

*—Genesis 4:9*

## A READING FROM OUR FAMILY BIBLE

1. Now the birth of the sons of Cain was in this wise.

**The First Son**

2. There was a certain man by the name of Cain. Paul, son of Patrick, was he named. And he took to wife Mary, daughter of Johanna. And Paul knew his wife Mary. And, though they were righteous before God, walking in all the commandments and, in ordinances of the Lord, blameless, still they were grieved and sore beset because, after six years of marriage, no children did they have.

3. Now, as neither of them was getting any younger, to a doctor they did go who decreed that a child they would have if Mary should quit her good-paying job. This she did and lo! it happened as he had foretold. She did conceive and bear a son, who was called Paul after his father, though Paul Francis he was called and

81

not Paul Vincent lest the child should be called Junior.

4.  And all the relatives did bring presents. Booties were brought and sweaters. And so happy were his parents that announcements were put in the paper. In both editions of the paper were they put. Morning and evening was this birth proclaimed. And great was the joy that greeted this long-awaited child.

5.  Paul grew in spirit; he waxed strong in body and the grace of God was on him.

### The Journey from Home

6.  And it came to pass that there was no work in the land. Then, in a dream, an angel did appear to the father, saying, "Arise and take the child and his mother and flee into New York where you will find a job." And when the husband told this dream unto his wife, she did say, "Let's pack." And pack they did.

7.  And the father's family did accuse the mother harshly, saying "Mary, you are breaking up the Cain family. Let your husband stay in Syracuse where he will work in the Golden Lion." (Now the Golden Lion was the father's eldest brother's saloon, and a good saloon it was, and many are the stories told thereof.) But Mary did say No, that her husband would be the biggest drunk in Syracuse if he did remain.

8.  So Paul and Mary went out from the embrace of their families and fled into the wilderness of New York. And Mary said, "Our neighbors must be our family now."

9.  And it was as Mary had said. Their neighbors were their family. The Gomezes, the McDonalds, and all the others who had left their families to find work in New York became family unto one another. And Mr. and Mrs. Bietta, who were two hundred years old and spoke with Italian accents, and Cockney Granny, deaf from working in the British mills, were as grandparents to all the children. And Nat and Lou, who ran the candy store on the corner and had num-

bers tattooed on their wrists, were as uncles. And Bobby Lee who fought in Korea and returned unharmed (which much astonished the children who thought that anyone who went to war needs must die) was as a cousin. And a large family it was.

## On the Difficulty of Having a Large Family

10. And having such a large family was sometimes hard for the children. Since everyone in the neighborhood did know to whom each child belonged, they couldn't get away with very much without their parents hearing about it. Fast.

## The Second Son

11. And the large family became larger still. For another son was born to Paul and Mary, a brother unto the first, and the name given him was William. And when his birth was announced, his uncle Robert, a father of six, said wearily, "Oh, that second child!" thus prophesying that the second child was to be more difficult than was the first. And indeed it was as he had said.

12. Colicky he was, and difficult was his teething. And once he actually turned blue, thus scaring the bejeezus out of his father. And for years his parents could not understand his speech. A child of dreams, and visions was he, and so different was he from his brother that his mother did say unto her husband, "I don't know, Pete. Maybe we got the wrong baby at the hospital."

13. But the older brother did understand the younger brother's speech well and did interpret his words for him, and there was no silence between them. And together they grew and all rites and ceremonies of growing up were duly observed and the elder was indeed the younger brother's keeper.

## "Sure"

14. And each year, great was the celebration of Christmas, for the mother was zealous that the perfect gifts should be

given. So when the elder son was old enough for the gift of the bicycle, a two-wheeler was given, though the parents had to take out a loan from the bank to manage it.

15.   And when the younger brother wanted a ride on the back of the elder's bike, he would ask and his brother would say, "Sure." And truly, at such moments, the elder brother was as a god unto the younger.

## A Father's Words

16.   And as the elder boy did grow, his father instructed him in all the lessons of manhood. "Be a catcher," he did say. "Baseball teams always need catchers." And a catcher he became. And a cross-country runner as well, for he was fleet of foot.

17.   And, strong in body, at thirteen to military school did he go, and then to college, and then into the army, for he felt he must fill up the need of the family for a soldier since his father in the Second World War did not fight.

## The Beginning of Sorrows

18.   To Alaska first he did go, where the earthquake he did withstand, for it had been foretold in the scriptures that there should be earthquakes in diverse places and these are but the beginning of sorrows. For nation shall rise against nation and kingdom against kingdom. And it was indeed so, for it was 1967 and unto Vietnam did the young lieutenant go, a warrior to become.

## The Brothers and War

19.  And when the younger son was thirteen and it was time for him to go to high school, he did follow in his brother's footsteps to military school. But follow him to Vietnam he did not. And while the elder brother's hair was shaved, the younger's hair grew long. Priestcraft he did study, and a priest he did become, anointed with all the sacred oils.

20.   For still was he subject to dreams and visions, and these visions did not include a land war in Southeast Asia. Carpet

bombing they did not include, nor napalm. Neither did they include the invasion of Cambodia nor Operation Rolling Thunder.

21. So while the elder marched in the jungle, the younger marched in the streets. And while the older did, from his perspective, risk his life to protect the younger's right to protest, the younger did, from his perspective, protest the war that put his brother's life at risk. And, in general, they went through life canceling each other out.

22. And the elder did send letters home. Fifty-one letters did he send. But they are their own story and deserve time and space to tell their own secrets.

## The Father and War

23. And as the battles raged that terrible year, the father tried to follow the progress of his son's war as he had followed wars in times past. With a map on the wall and pins he tried to follow the front. But this war had no front. Nor back. Nor top nor bottom.

"Men are poured into this bottomless war without sense," said the younger son to the father, and the father was exceeding wroth and would shout, "But your brother's in this war!" And the younger son would shout back, "But look at the pins and see what they tell you!" For pins came and went and there was no sense to it, and such was the progress of this war.

## The Mother and War

24. And the family did celebrate Christmas sadly that year, and with many prayers, for the elder son was far away and in danger. Presents were exchanged, but the most important presents had been sent, long before, by the mother to Vietnam. Carefully wrapped in coffee cans were they sent. A Christmas tree and all the trimmings the mother had sent, so that the feast of peace might be celebrated even in midst of war.

## And New Year's

25. And the New Year did follow Christmas. And the New

Year was also celebrated in Vietnam and the name for New Year in Vietnam is Tet.

## The Welcome Home

26. And, after a year, when the soldier was to return home, his father, in great joy, lettered a banner and hung it from the fire escape for all to see. And the banner said, "WELCOME HOME, PAUL!"

27. But welcomed he was not. For when he got off the plane that brought him home, a protestor threw an egg at him and called him "Baby killer." And this did not help the relationship between the brothers one bit.

28. And from that time, there was between the brothers a great gulf fixed. Though they were always friendly, they were not really friends.

29. And the friendly distance between the brothers felt so great that sometimes the younger wondered if, after the death of the parents, he and his brother would even stay in touch.

## 'It's Alright"

30. For the war did set its mark on Cain.

31. And he who used to interpret for his brother could now scarcely interpret for himself. "No problem," he would say. Or "It's alright."

32. But there was a problem and nothing was alright.

33. His hearing was less because of the artillery fire he had heard. Thirty percent less it was. And when he was out walking with his mother and a loud noise was heard, he would jump into the street and roll under a car. And troubling was this to his parents and worried were they for him.

34. Of the first Cain it was said "He shall be a fugitive and vagabond on the earth." Likewise, Paul Francis Cain went out from the presence of his parents and did dwell in deserts of the Southwest where, at the army's request, he did get a master's degree in math that he might more effi-

ciently calculate the destruction of the world.

35. And he drank and he was not happy.

36. Three times did he try to leave the army, though his mother and father objected, saying, "Stay for the pension. It's only eight more years." But his wife did wisely say, "If you're not happy, what's the point?" For he had married; a nurse named Janet he had married. And they had a child, a beautiful girl called Nancy who brought joy to all. "If you're not happy," said Janet, "do something else. We'll get by."

37. And Paul left the army. Day and night he worked to support his family. In a restaurant he did work by day and in a 7-Eleven by night.

## A Father's Last Words

38. When it came time for the father to go the way of all the earth, his last words to Mary, his wife, were "Look after Paul." "Look after Paul," he did say.

39. And although the mother wished to look after Paul, she did not know how. They talked on the phone and spent Christmases together rejoicing as Nancy grew in wisdom, age, and grace. But still there was a distance between them.

## Looking After Paul

40. Many years later, when the mother grew old and wished to make distribution of her goods, she decided to give to the elder son the best thing she owned. Now the best thing she owned was her car, for not only was it her most valuable possession, it was also her freedom. And, when it came time for her to give her freedom up, she made a virtue of her necessity. After much thought, and mindful of her husband's words, she called her elder son and said "Paul, could you use a car?"

41. "Could I!" said Paul. For Paul was now a math teacher, using for creation what he had been taught for destruction. And, though he was a nationally recognized teacher, yet

was he living on a teacher's salary. It was for this reason that, when his mother said "Could you use a car," he answered, "Could I!"

42. But he was worried, for truly he did not want to deprive his mother of her freedom. And neither did he have the means to make the trip to come and get the car.

43. But his mother did assure him that it was indeed time for her to give up her freedom. And when the younger brother offered him the means to make the trip, he did fly to Syracuse, plans having been made for him to drive the car back across the country. Even unto El Paso would he drive the car. For five days, alone would he drive.

44. And the younger brother, now a teacher as well, confident that the elder would say "No," asked if he could come along for the ride. And the elder did call the younger's bluff by saying, "Sure."

45. Thus a great adventure began.

## The Trip Back

46. And as the brothers were packing the car to leave on the trip, the mother was sore distressed, for she was old and thought she might never see her elder son again. So, as he was leaving, the mother embraced him and did say with many tears, "Goodbye, Paul." And into the car did the elder brother go. Then she embraced the younger son, and did say with as many tears, "Goodbye, Billy." And into the car did the younger brother go.

47. Then the mother did speak again. Soft and low did she speak, for she did not want her sons to hear her words.

48. When she spoke, unto the car did she speak. And with tears equal to those she had shed for her sons, she said, "Goodbye, car."

49. But her sons did hear their mother speak unto the car with as much affection as she had spoken to them. And they did laugh. Heartily they did laugh. And so did the mother along with them as she said

goodbye to her beloved sons and her even more beloved car.

50. Thus the trip began. And in laughter did it begin.

## Together

51. Long had it been since the brothers had laughed together. Or spent a full day together. Or traveled together. And though there were awkward silences between them, both knew that it was indeed good that they were together.

## The Wall

52. Together, on the evening of the first day, the brothers arrived in Washington, DC, where is the Wall. And on this wall are the names of those who died in the war in Vietnam. And the first duty the brothers did feel on arriving in the city was to visit the Wall, where the elder had never yet been.

53. So, as the sun was setting, to the Wall they went, the elder stopping once to go back to the hotel. "I have to get my

medals," he said. Then, with medals in hand, again they set out for the Wall.

54. In silence they went. And the younger said to the elder, "I'm nervous." And the elder said, "Don't worry. I'm not going to scream or do anything crazy." And the younger said, "I'm not worried about you." And on in silence did they go until they arrived at the Wall.

55. The younger arrived first, yet he paused. He let his brother precede him into the valley wherein the Wall sits. Slowly the elder moved forward, and the fear of God was upon him. And in silence he beheld the endless names of those who had died in the war.

56. As the elder went deeper into the valley, the younger brother followed close, watching. And he saw his brother begin to shake as if wrestling with a man within him to see who was the stronger.

57. Shake he did. And sigh. And as he struggled to speak,

spirits came out of him and rent him sore.

58. He did not say, "No problem" or "It's alright." This time he said, "Get me out of here. I can't breathe."

### Nevers

59. As they left, they stopped by the statue of The Three Soldiers and the elder brother was sore beset. "I have to sit down," he said. And as they sat, the elder, with much feeling, said, "It's just like Vietnam. I'm glad I was there, but I never want to go back again. Never."

60. But as they left the precinct area, the elder asked a fellow soldier, now heavy of body and selling t-shirts, "What time does the Wall close?" And he did answer, "Never."

### A Burger and Fries

61. The younger, moved with much feeling for his brother, took him to Union Station to dine. "Order whatever you want; this is on me," he said.

And the elder said unto the waitress, "I want a hamburger and fries." And the younger insisted, "No, have something good." And the elder said again, with anger now, "A burger and fries," and they spoke no more until a burger and fries were delivered unto him. And as he began to eat he did say, "For a full year in Vietnam, all I wanted was a burger and fries."

62. And as they ate, the brothers did talk about many things, but about the Wall they did not speak a word.

63. It grew late. Near midnight it was as they left Union Station, when the elder said, as the younger had hoped he would, "Let's go back."

64. And they did go back. And it was night. And Paul wept. Silently, facing the Wall, did he weep.

65. "I belong here," he said. "I brought my ribbons and medals, but I didn't need to. I keep them to remind me, but I don't need them here. I belong here."

## The Transfiguration of
## the Elder

66. And when they walked out of the valley of the Wall to face again the Three Soldiers, the elder was transfigured before them. His face did shine like the sun and he did smile at the bronze soldiers even as the tears ran down his face.

67. Like a man seeing friends long missing and presumed dead, did he smile, did he cry. And his face was bright as light.

## Of Colors and Wonders

68. Talk of the soldiers he did. He spoke of them as friends and he bade the younger to mark them well. He said, "It's entirely different at night. Look, you can see this one is blond and that one has dark hair." And he went on speaking of the wonder of the colors he saw.

69. But the younger brother could see no colors. It seemed to him that the statues were bronze and nothing more. He could see no wonder there.

No wonder, that is, but his brother.

70. And the younger brother said, "I want to take a picture," for he wist not what he said. And as the elder moved in front of the statue for a picture, all others at the statue moved away and left him alone before the Soldiers. For the elder spake true when he said he belonged there and all others saw it and let him stand there alone.

71. And proudly he stood with the Three Soldiers. And transfigured he was in the eyes of all. Even in his own eyes was he transfigured.

## Brothers

72. Before the brothers went to bed that night, the first night they would sleep in the same room since they were children, they spoke in fits and starts. Haltingly they spoke, since the silence between them was charged with much feeling.

73. And the elder said, "I want to thank you for making

this trip possible for me...."
And younger said, "No, no,
no, no, thank you for the
honor of letting me be with
you when..." And again the
elder, "No, no, no, don't...."

74.   And, for an unexpected
moment, the brothers found
themselves in each other's
arms. Not as in an embrace on
meeting or parting. But as in
an endless reaching for one
another. And the brothers
who had been lost to each
other were found again. In
each other's arms they were
found.

75.   The wide circles that had
carried them so far from one
another had carried them back
to one another.

76.   And it was morning and
evening on the first day.

### Necessary Words

77.   The following morning the
elder went to the Wall alone,
where he met other soldiers.

78.   And one of these soldiers
said to him the necessary words.
He said, "Welcome Home."

### The Trip Continues

79.   As they journeyed across
the country, the brothers
talked. The silence between
them was broken and they
talked. How they talked!

80.   They bypassed all the
cities and paid little attention
to the country, for there was
too much geography in the car
already as they shared the
journeys of their lives.

81.   And every day they visited
Vietnam.

### "Nothing I Could Do"

82.   And the elder did speak
unto the younger. And once he
began to speak, there was no
end to what needed saying.

83.   He spoke of days when it
rained fire and brimstone from
heaven. Of days when two
men shall be in the field; the
one shall be taken, and the
other left.

84.   He spoke of landing a
plane when he did not know
how and of how fast you can
learn when your pilot has

been shot. Of medals that cause more trouble than they are worth.

85. Sometimes in another language he spoke. Of mad minutes, rear echelon motherfuckers, of the Parrot's Beak and of gravel agitators he spoke.

86. He spoke about the impossibility of speaking about what he had seen.

## Vicksburg

87. And the brothers talked so much that they drove across the Mississippi without noticing it, which did not seem right. So they drove back to cross it again. And, as they got out to see the mighty river, they rested on an ancient cannon that faced the river, memorial to another war that had set brother against brother.

88. So much did they enjoy each other's company that the closer they got to their destination, the slower they drove. Indeed, they did extend the trip another day.

## One More Story

89. And even so, at the city limits of El Paso, the elder brother said unto the younger, "There's more." He said, "There's another story."

90. And, as he drove slowly through the side streets of El Paso, the elder brother told his final story.

91. And, finally, he spoke of sorrow.

92. He spoke of a terrifying Halloween night ambush and of how it had ruined Halloween for him forever.

93. For he was as a man under authority, having soldiers under him, and he said to this man go and he goeth and to another come and he cometh.

94. And one of those men was his college roommate and he spoke of how this college roommate died under his command. Yards from him he died. Yea, even as he was speaking to him on the radio did his life fade away. "And

there was nothing I could do," the elder brother said.

95.    "There was nothing I could do."

96.    And, with all the stories finally told, they drove on in silence.

97.    And home at last he was.

### Christmas

98.    So it didn't really matter if, on her last Christmas, the mother could place but few gifts under the tree, though it bothered the hell out of her that, for once, she would get more than she would give. But it really didn't matter, for this year, in giving the car, a great gift was given.

99.    For each brother gave himself unto the other.

100.    And the brothers became once again what the children of Cain must always be. Finally and, I believe, forever—it is the younger brother who writes this— each became his brother's keeper.

### Chapter 8. The Sons of Cain

The story of siblings gets off to a bad start in the Bible. Our namesake, Cain, and his brother Abel, have a disagreement that ends badly for both of the siblings. Things don't get much better as the story goes on with Jacob (the favored child) stealing the elder brother's—Esau's—birthright. And then there is Joseph and his coat of many colors. His brothers first plot to kill him and then sell him into slavery.

Can there be any revelation in siblinghood?

Well, perhaps not for Cain and Abel, but after Jacob wrestled with an angel and had his hip put out of joint, he attempted a reconciliation with Esau. And, most hopefully, there is the story of the reunion of Joseph and his brothers—

*Joseph said to his brothers, "I am Joseph!...* "Come close to me." ... *And he kissed all his brothers and wept over them.*

So perhaps there is hope for revelation among biblical siblings after all. Though Joseph does warn them as he sends them back to Israel, *"Don't quarrel on the way!"*

As I once said to my brother when asked what the function of a family was—a family is a crucible to turn passion into love.

It doesn't always work.

But sometimes—I hope most times—we have improved on the Bible.

## 9

# The Liturgy of the Hours

---

### New Year's to Ash Wednesday
#### JANUARY 1 – FEBRUARY 16

New Year's resolutions have never been very helpful to me.

I never had much luck with giving things up for Lent either.

Until I made a success of my failures by combining them.

Now I make as many New Year's resolutions as I want, keep them till Ash Wednesday, then I give them up for Lent.

It works. I recommend it.

Even so, I made only one resolution this year.

**January 1.** Resolution: Facing one of the great mysteries—death—make each day as deeply felt and richly lived as possible. Let time reveal its mysteries. And write about it. Note it. Treasure it every moment.

Nice thought. However, my entire diary entry for January 2nd was:

Nothing happened.

Well, that resolution didn't last long.

It disturbs me to see how many of my diary entries for this period are similar.

**January 4.** Mom ate an egg.

Can that be all that happened that day?

To be fair, it was a dark, cold, sleepy time—the middle of a horrendous winter. Maybe nothing did happen. It would be consoling to think so. Otherwise I would just have to admit I didn't think whatever was happening in the apartment was worth noting.

My diary for this period, though, is not blank.

On the contrary. It is full of annotations about my work, a script I was trying to get out by February 15th—the day before Ash Wednesday. As the deadline approached I worked on the script practically round the clock and all the last-minute changes are duly noted in my diary.

Now, looking back, I realize that you don't have to be far away to be far away. Though I was in the house, I conspired —and perhaps Mom did too—in this lonely time to preserve our individual lonelinesses.

Why?

Why did I abandon my resolution to appreciate what was going on around me?

Was it that I found simply being there hard? Demanding in a way for which I do not have a talent? When medical tests were going on, I felt purposeful, of use, important. But somehow, when there was no crisis, when I was simply keeping my mother company, I felt very exposed, foolish even. Now I wish I had just a few dull notes on every uneventful day. But I don't. So, nothing, it seems, happened from New Year's Day to Ash Wednesday. For forty-seven days. Nothing. Or little.

Who knows?

Maybe, out of memories and my few diary annotations, I can put together one complete day.

It's worth a try.

———

Through sleep, I hear the start of her day dimly.

Mom talks quietly, not quite to herself, as she goes through the dark house, turning on lights, touching important objects—photos, statues, significant toys, and saying *Good Morning* to them.

First, she touches the feet of a crucifix that was a wedding present from the priest that married her and her Pete. She says with a piety I find embarrassing, *Good morning, my Jesus.* Then, less reverently, cheerfully even, as she raises the shades, she says *Good morning* to a worn wooden statue of St. Francis of Assisi. (She has a businesslike relationship with God, but she and Francis are old friends. If any of her friends are traveling today, she will place St. Francis in the window to look after them.) Then, as she touches the heads of chipped dime-store plaster statues of St. Patrick and the Virgin Mary, *Good morning, good morning.* ... Several dolls are greeted, including a musical one named Bridget after a neighbor's child in New York who is confined to a wheelchair after a teen-age car accident. *Good morning, my Bridget.* Then, with a laugh, shaking her head at the size of it, she greets an enormous teddy bear she named Cuddles.

She then touches any number of photographs of family —especially her granddaughter *Good morning, Nancy*—and friends, with updated photos jammed into the edges of the frames. Finally, she greets formal college portraits of my brother and me, wishing us each *Good morning, Paul. Good morning, Billy.*

(There is no picture of my father. I find that disturbing.)
The kettle whistles. Her day has begun.
I turn over and go back to sleep.
The morning paper is retrieved from the hall.

Before it is read, a dirty old envelope full of memorial cards, battered old medals, prayers clipped from newspapers, and other flotsam of a spiritual life is emptied onto the kitchen table. And, as she sips her first cup of tea, she prays. This takes time—an hour?—it's too early for me to know exactly. It takes time because she prays for everybody: family, friends living and deceased, the nations of the world, the souls in purgatory and, finally, in a self-contradictory way, she prays for everybody who has nobody to pray for them. As a kid this used to bother me. *But Mom, if you're praying for them...*

Over a second cup of tea, she reads the paper thoroughly. *Tsk, tsk, tsk...Oh, my, would you look at that....* At eight o'clock on the dot, the phone rings (this call is the beginning of my day) and it is Mom's friend, Paulette. Without greeting, they begin discussing the paper. *Well, did you see on page 6....Isn't it terrible?* There will be many more calls from Paulette during the day and none will begin with a hello. She and Mom are in the middle of a conversation that has been going on for years. *Did you see the changes in Social Security on page nine?*

A slow waker-up, I stagger into the kitchen shortly after Mom hangs up. Over a cup of tea and a bagel, Mom and I chat. She will be full of questions. *How late did you stay up? Did anybody call? Did the writing go well?* I will tell her how badly the writing went and she will tell me *Nonsense.* And we talk on. Pain management will be part of this conversation, but usually the morning is not a time for pain. In many ways this quiet morning talk is the best part of the day. And what do we talk about?

Everything.

Nothing.

Certainly nothing I have written down.

I work on the morning crossword puzzle which Mom will have begun. Even if no words are written in, Mom, always slow to fill in *across* without being certain of *down*, has already started. I'm the opposite of Mom in this and write in the first answer that comes to mind. After my pass, Mom will take over again, and erase half, but she will also leave half, so there's a net gain. If we didn't manage to finish the puzzle from the day before, Mom will inform me of what we missed. *That 11-down yesterday was "wallop."* As Mom takes over the puzzle (now with her well-worn puzzle dictionaries) I grind up pain pills for her, hoping they will ensure a peaceful day. With a toothpick I remove the paper that covers each pill to allow easier swallowing.

Then, with the next cup of tea, I go to the back room. This is my best writing time, before I'm awake enough to get in my own way. *You go along, Billy, I'm alright,* and she is. In the next few hours, she will take her medications (thyroid, heart, and pain), write cards to friends and family (all birthdays and anniversaries remembered), watch TV or nap, *I'm just going to close my eyes for a minute, Billy.* I will check in on her every twenty minutes or so, every time I fix a new cup of tea.

Unless it's a day she goes to Gloria to get her hair done—*I don't know how many more times I can do that, Billy*—the morning is usually quiet.

As I said . . . nothing happens.

————

Mid-morning, four days a week, either Cathy or Carol will arrive.

When my mother's cleaning-lady-and-psychotherapist Cathy arrives, Mom will have the kettle simmering so the tea water will be ready the instant Cathy lets herself in with a timid *Hello?* Mom, delighted and somehow surprised, will say *Well, look who's here!* Mom never had a daughter, but, two days a week, she does have Cathy. And they sit and laugh and chat quietly over their tea in flowered mugs. Nothing big. Cathy's bowling scores. Sales. The weather. And, endlessly, the complications of their lives with their children and husbands.

(I thought Cathy best summarized the complications of family once when I asked her what kind of books she liked. With a glint in her eye she answered that she used to read *Romance*, but ever since her eighteenth wedding anniversary, she'd switched to *True Crime*.)

The chief topic with Carol is also family.

Carol, older and more seasoned than Cathy, has remarkable resilience for all the serious sickness she has seen her family through. (She is currently taking care of one of her daughters during a difficult pregnancy.) But nothing seems to get her down. I have never heard Carol complain, and she has had cause.

Carol cooks for Mom, an odd activity since Mom doesn't eat. Because Mom loves Carol's company, every day she tosses out a bit of what Carol has prepared so that Carol can keep coming and cooking, a solution worthy of a Zen master, or, better, since I think Carol is on to it, two Zen masters.

Both Cathy and Carol are generous spirits and somehow the chaos that they bring to the house with their cooking and cleaning makes the house seem more peaceful than it does in total quiet. Both of them do their jobs very well, but their work is only a good excuse to enjoy their healing company.

**January 28.** The streets are too icy for Cathy to
come. Cathy not coming to clean leaves a big hole
in the day.

**February 2.** No Carol today. The house is very very
lonely.

———

Noon—and we all stop to watch the news.

The women follow the problems of the world with compassion, local politics with disdain, sports with passion.

Then, news over, activity resumes—cleaning and cooking and writing and sleeping—as we all go our separate
ways again.

———

As the day goes on, there might be guests.

Paulette might come by. *I got you some stockings, Mary, the
kind you like. They were on sale so don't WORRY about it.* Or
Mom's niece, Mary Lou, whom Mom enjoys so much she
pays her the ultimate compliment: *She's just like me when I was
her age.* Mary Lou will inevitably have packets of old photos
of Mom's growing up. Fr. Paul, hale, hearty, and a bit false,
will come by to deliver Communion. And Mom will visit
with them all and they will talk and talk about not-a-hell-of-
a-lot since nothing has happened since the last visit.

———

Helen, another of Mom's friends, might come by.

When Helen comes, she comes empty-handed. No
magazine to read. No knitting. She just arrives. And Helen

never expects to be entertained. On the contrary, when she arrives, she sends me out. *You must have things to do* (and I do). When I return and ask how things are going, if Mom and Helen are talking, Helen will say. *Oh, your mother and I are just having a nice visit.* If, when I return, Helen is sitting at the foot of Mom's bed with Mom fast asleep and I ask how things are, Helen will say, *Oh, your mother and I are just having a nice visit.*

Nothing happens, but Helen makes of nothing something very impressive. When I try to ask Helen about this, or try to compliment her on it, she honestly doesn't know what I am talking about.

––––––

On a good afternoon, Mom will watch the talk shows and stay current on news bulletins.

> **January 28.** A snow storm was the event of the day and Mom followed it all over the country.

*They had to close the airport in Denver, Billy. Those poor people...*
On a bad afternoon we wrestle with pain.

––––––

There are many, many diary entries about pain.

> Bad pain day.... Pain all afternoon.... Good day
> with an hour of pain in the middle ruining it all

...and there are other entries where the pain takes over as in this uncharacteristically long annotation from January 26:

Today was the worst pain yet.

I know it was bad because Mom asked me to rub
her back to relieve the pain...and that is something
she would never under other circumstances do.

She let me help her from the living room to the
kitchen again and again...And you can hear the
pain in her voice. Under every sound is the voice of
a child saying *make it stop*.

Finally I told her just to take more pain medication and fixed her what amounted to an extra dose
for the day.

She didn't want to be alone so I spent most of
the day with her.

When she was going to bed I asked her to get
me up early because I hadn't gotten much done during the day.

She said, *Yes, you did. You took care of me*, and
went to bed.

But I must not have believed her because I stayed up till
two a.m. writing.

———

After my mother has spent endless tours in the apartment
trying to walk out the pain, the medication will finally take
hold and she will sleep, but the day is never the same after
that. A nap will not restore peace like a night of sleep will.
Winter afternoons are lonely and long and will be interrupted only by a short trip to the mailbox if Mom is up for
it. When she is not up to it, she pesters me to *Check the mail,
check the mail,* which is annoying because there is never
much in the mail. Bills that will be paid instantaneously. Cir-
culars. Donation-soliciting letters that will be thoroughly

read and considered. And, usually, a personal note or two. Mom and her friends frequently send one another Hallmark "To a Special Friend" cards, personalizing the verse by underlining specific words, for emphasis...(To a Special Friend). Mom can read a card a dozen times and be moved by it every time. It is a rare day that Mom does not hear from a friend.

Of all Mom's correspondents, my favorite is Jane Dunsmore because, though they are good friends, they have never met.

Margaret Stevenson was a good friend of Mom's, and Mom heard so much about Margaret's sister Jane that she wrote to her, and now, long after Margaret has died, their correspondence goes on. I think that's nice.

---

Evening news, the evening paper with a new crossword puzzle, and dinner, most of which will, of course, be thrown away.

After dinner, television.

Mom will hunt for the Knicks to root them forward in a season when it looks like they could go all the way.

TV will be interrupted by phone calls. Paul from Texas, Kevin from California, Miriam in New York, Grey or Khorshed in Boston, Marjorie in Connecticut...from all over, really...friends of mine and friends of hers. We don't talk about much. What is there to talk about on a snowy dark day? We just pass the time.

After the ten o'clock news (always from New York City to check up on the city she loves) the day begins to end.

We go back to the kitchen table (where we started) and if we haven't solved the morning puzzle, we have another go at it. If we can't complete it, she'll clip it. *We'll have to check that 12 down tomorrow morning. That was a stinker.* If she does finish it, she'll say *Give me an A* and I'll put a great big A on the paper.

And we review the day. Who we saw, who we talked to. Who called. Who didn't. What tomorrow's going to be like.

We talk about pain and medications. If it's been a rough day she will ask me to leave my door open a crack so if she needs me, she can call in the night, though she never does.

Then one final ritual.

Mom reverses what she did in the morning and says good night to her little model of the universe.

*Good night* to the crucifix, the saints, the dolls.

*Good night* to the photos, statues, and toys.

*Good night* to the teddy bear.

*Good night* to her granddaughter and her boys.

Then she'll say to me, *Don't stay up too late,* and she'll go to bed.

———

So—

Nothing much happened.

Just looking in on all the nations of the world several times,

talking to both coasts and many cities in between,

fighting through really terrible pain and taking inordinate joy in very simple pleasures.

After some loneliness and much friendship,

the day ends.

**January 4:** Mom ate an egg.

Nothing much happened most days.

And I wish I had more of it written down.

### Chapter 9. Liturgy of the Hours

**Liturgy of the Hours (Set of 4) Bonded Leather—
by International Commission on English in the Liturgy.**
*Printed in two colors in large 14-pt. type and bound in bonded leather,
this complete four-volume set of the Liturgy of the Hours includes
handy ribbon markers and features a gold-stamped spine and elegant
gilded page edging. Sold only as a set. Bonded Leather. $207.00*
*—Entry on Amazon*

Monks chant the liturgy of the hours—maybe even out of
a bonded leather, four-volume prayerbook set.

It's part of the ritual of a monastery.

But I believe every house is a fully functioning monastery.

With its rituals and practices.

With work and recreation.

With fasting and feasting.

With penances and communions.

The rituals might not have been written down in bonded
leather, with handy ribbon markers and elegant gilded
page edging.

But they are there. In every home.

Waiting to be claimed.

Prayed for free.

Waiting to be written down and shared.

*Do not go gentle into that good night,*
*Old age should burn and rave at close of day;*
*Rage, rage against the dying of the light.*
    — *Dylan Thomas*

## 10

# What Does Dylan Thomas Know about It Anyway?

### *Prayer—Part 1*

Prayer.

People think prayer is something you do when you are totally still. Why? Why is kneeling—immobile—the traditional prayer position? The more immobile, the more

prayerful? Why don't we think of movement as prayer as well? For example, here is a picture of my brother that strikes me as being prayerful in the extreme.

Paul is high school cross-country captain, and his feet aren't even touching the ground as he runs for the finish line. Why is this act of totally self-forgetful self-giving not every bit as much prayer as kneeling in a church pew, perfectly still, hands folded?

OK. Maybe the only reason I think momentum is prayer is that it's so hard for me to be utterly still. Witness

my favorite picture of myself ever—as I'm about to pick up speed sliding down the snowy hill behind Uncle Bobby's house.

I am older now, but I think some part of me still looks exactly like that and that part of me is called my soul. And— maybe because that's the shape

of my soul—I think that prayer has a momentum of its own.

In their prime, Mom and Dad both had tremendous momentum to them.

I'd put their wedding picture in here somewhere, but there isn't one.

They eloped.

Momentum.

The weekend they were to be married, they drove from Syracuse to New York in a legendarily destructive 1938 hurricane without paying it much attention. *Well, it was raining, but we figured we could make it. We didn't know how bad it was till we drove over a bridge and there was a crowd standing on the other side, just standing there in the rain. So Pete rolled down the window and asked them what they were doing and they told him they were waiting for the bridge to wash out. Imagine! But we couldn't stop. Fr. Edmund was waiting for us at the monastery. How could we stop?*

———

And they never did.

If they said they'd be there, they'd be there. For each other, for their kids, for their friends. They met planes, trains, buses and boats. Attended track meets, debate tournaments, plays, dances, PTA meetings, baptisms, birthday parties, confirmations, weddings, retirement diners, funerals.... Their inevitable presence has seriously disabled me in one way. It makes no sense at all to me when my friends tell me that their parents missed an event. I have no way to understand that. Carried on a lifetime habit of endless momentum, my parents were *always* there.

―――――

Mom still has considerable momentum of her own. More in fact than she can handle.

Mom's solution to the fact that she is barely able to walk is to run. If, while she is napping, the phone rings, she will leap up from the bed or the couch and, wildly unsteady, run for the phone. If she has an attack of back pain on the way, she will lurch and stagger as if she'd been shot in the back by a sniper, but she will *not* slow down. When I tell her I am frightened that she is going to fall, *Well, if I fall, I fall* is her only response.

Though I admire her drive, it also pisses me off. The risks that she is taking are eventually going to cause me trouble. So, parental (*This is for your own good, Mom*), and over her strong objections, I make an appointment for a physical therapist to do an in-home evaluation of Mom, hoping that, since she won't listen to me, she will listen to a therapist and start using the obviously necessary cane or walker.

The therapist, an earnest, humorless man in his thirties, arrives.

I greet him at the door and bring him into the living room. My mother, who normally has to struggle to get up from the couch and fight for her balance to lurch into the kitchen, now rises from that same couch in one effortless finishing-school motion, and, smiling, walks smoothly toward the therapist, holding out a steady hand to shake his.

The therapist is much impressed.

So, frankly, am I. All I could think was, *Who is this lady and what has she done with my mother?*

The therapist sets about his work giving Mom a series of tests to evaluate her strength. *Now, Mrs. Cain . . .*

*Call me Mary...*

*Mary, if you'd just push your hand against mine. . . .* She presses; he yields. He presses until she must yield. Again and again and back and forth, and my mother, game, goes through several such tests with a perplexed look on her face. When the therapist finally notices Mom's bafflement and asks her what's wrong, she, amused but completely honest, says, *Well, I don't mind playing, but I can't tell who's winning.*

That was to become clear momentarily.

The therapist, kneeling in front of Mom, asks her to place her foot against his shoulder. This requires some effort on her part; bemusedly but willingly, she bends her knee and gets her foot up against his shoulder. The therapist then explains, speaking slowly, as if to a child, that he wants to test the strength in her legs, and if, when he gives the word, she'd just straighten her leg. . . .

Now I've seen enough comic routines to know what is going to happen. He, humorless, hasn't. *Well,* I think, *he's just going to learn the hard way.*

So, when he solemnly gives the sign, my mother takes a deep breath, straightens her leg abruptly and kicks the therapist across the room and into the table with her one good lamp on it.

After a brief pause to allow him to steady the lamp, Mom asks him happily, *How'd I do?*

As he is leaving, the therapist gives me his evaluation. It is not an evaluation of my mother. It is an evaluation of me.

I am clearly a good son but perhaps my concern for my mother is a bit alarmist. My mother nods sagely. As far as he can see there is no need, no need whatsoever, for a cane or a walker. My mother nods sagely. Mom thanks him for coming out on such a cold day and walks him, steadily, into the hall, where she waves him cheerfully on his way.

The instant the door is closed, Mom slumps against it. She then turns to me and says, *God, I'm tired. Billy. Please don't have any more people like that come to the house. They wear me out.*

Then she grabs the wall, staggers drunkenly into the bedroom and collapses on the bed.

She won't sleep long.

She'll be up and on the move soon.

———

But, when faced with a doctor's appointment, when I need Mom to move, Mom's irresistible momentum hits the immoveable object of her fear, resulting in a grim stillness.

So, for days before the appointment I work against her inertia. I urge, I cajole, I kid. *Come on, Mom, you can't call in sick for a doctor's appointment.* I look on the bright side. *At least you'll get out of the house. And Pat is going to drive us. You know how much you enjoy Pat.* I reason with her. I explain that blood work needs to be done, that we need to talk with the doctor about her increasingly frequent coughing spells (a hideous combination of choking and dry heaves) and, as always, the pain medication needs to be negotiated. But she will not move until I answer the question that, though never asked, is always present. *No matter what,* I say, *no matter what, I won't let the doctor put you in the hospital. No matter what he says, we will come back here.*

Then, finally, she moves.

She moves slowly, but she moves.

And once my mother has decided to move, she is relentless. From that point on, even though she will say under her breath, *This is the last time I will do this,* you can count on her. The habits of a lifetime will see her through. Shoe by shoe, hair by hair, snap by snap, she gets ready.

———

### JANUARY 6

Doctor's appointment today. 10 a.m.

From vital signs to farewell conversation, Mom will be in the doctor's office half an hour tops, but the preparation takes days. I've got a lot of sympathy for Mom. Imagine having to expend precious physical energy to go to see a doctor who you know for certain will never give you good news ever again. But I can't let sympathy slow me down. My job is to provide the momentum that will get Mom out the door because, frankly, *I* need her to see the doctor. I need the reassurance that we are moving in the right direction with her care. *Don't worry about that, Billy. You're doing a good job*, she says.

We are both up very early. More accurately, we have been up off and on all night since Mom wakes every few hours to wash a bit, dress a bit, sleep a bit. Mom's modesty forbids my helping her with this. She does one task at a time and lies down to rest in between, so by morning, she has already done a full day's work.

At nine, looking forward to Pat's usual cheery *I'll BE there!*, I call to confirm our ride. But there is no cheer to be had this morning. Instead, Pat offers a cautionary *Well, I'LL be there*, and then goes silent. Something's clearly wrong, but Pat, old-time polite, won't tell you when she thinks you're wrong. I try to be as direct as I can with Pat and she says, *Well, it is cold.*

This stops me.

Cold? Since this is turning out to be the coldest winter in Syracuse's history, this is not news. But, more importantly, it's not snowing and the roads are clear and I tell Pat this. *Yes,* she says seriously, *but it's very cold. Are you sure she's up for it?*

And I wonder.

Mom, pale but 90 percent ready to go, appears in the doorway. She has heard the hesitation in the rhythms of the phone call and walks into the kitchen. Sensing a potential break in the momentum, I get off the line immediately, telling Pat I'll call her right back.

*Does Pat think I shouldn't go?* she asks quietly.

Cheerleading, I tell Mom she looks great and ask if she needs any help. Since she doesn't, I urge her to go back into the bedroom to finish up. Mom nods in agreement, but she does not move.

Silence.

I ask her if there's anything wrong and she says no, but she still does not move.

Pause.

Then she holds out her hands which have been holding on to the back of the chair. *Look at me, Billy. I'm shaking like a leaf.*

And she is.

I nod in agreement, but tell her if she gets going, we can talk to the doctor about it.

And she does not move.

Then she smiles apologetically at me as if at a stranger.

The momentum is lost.

*What did Pat say?* she says in a voice that asks for honesty, so I answer honestly.

*Maybe I shouldn't go,* she says.

*The walk to the car is very short,* I say.

*Bill, I'm shaky.*

*I'll hold you up.*

*OK,* she agrees, but again she does not move. She wants to, but she cannot.

*Call Paulette and ask her if I should go.*

*No, Mom. Since when does Paulette make decisions for you? You decide.*

*Call the doctor and ask if I should go.*

*I'll call and cancel if you want, but I won't call and ask. Don't put me in that position.*

*I don't want to inconvenience him.*

*You won't inconvenience him one way or another. He'll be grateful for the time. If you don't want to go, that's all you have to say.*

*I'm going to call Paulette.*

*Talk to me. Tell me what you're thinking.*

*Call Paulette and ask her what I should do.*

*You call Paulette.*

And she says *I will* but she doesn't and we go around and around and around....

Finally Mom sits down and says, *I'm so confused. I am so confused.*

And she is, and her confusion is new and frightening to me.

What is going on?

Mary Cain has never had a problem deciding to do anything in her life.

Never.

So why this problem now deciding to...

———

Suddenly things become clear to me.

I begin to see that Mom is having a problem because—really—she isn't deciding to do something.

No.

On the contrary, she is deciding *not* to do something. And, for her, that is much, much harder. In fact, she has no experience doing it. At all. She is trying to decide to pass something by.

She is doing the unthinkable.

Mary Dawson Cain—winner of perfect attendance awards from every year of school—is deciding not to show up.

And that's hard.

Because, put simply, that's what dying is.

Not showing up any more.

And, against the habit of a lifetime, that's what she's trying to do.

And she says, *Help me, Billy.*

And I don't know what to say.

I know what she *wants* me to say. She wants me to say, *Stay home.* She wants me to say it because it is an unthinkable thought for her. She wants my permission not to show up. She wants me to say it's okay to give up. To stop. To miss the appointment. And that is, I know, the right thing to say. And I don't say it.

Silence.

Then—

*Help me, Billy.*

She is asking my permission to die...not all at once...but just a little bit. Just for today.

And now it is my turn not to be able to move.

Anger paralyzes me.

I find myself raging, feeling perhaps as Dylan Thomas did when he wrote a poem I learned when I was young and have always loved since, urging his father to *Rage, rage against the dying of the light.*

And I will be of no help to my mother from this point forward because it suddenly becomes insanely important to me that she make it to the doctor's appointment this morning.

Silence.

*Help me, Billy.*

And it occurs to me—for the first time really—that my mother's dying is not a matter of indifference to me. This may seem absurdly obvious, but it wasn't. In some ways I hadn't really thought much about her dying. My focus had been almost entirely on keeping her alive. Keeping the momentum going. And I had been doing that so well that it suddenly seems like a betrayal for her to ask to stop. And, as it occurs to me slowly that my real job is helping her not to live, but to die, I become aware that I have no idea how to do that. Or that I want to. Or can.

And we sit in silence for a moment.

I say, *It's your call, Mom.*

And she says, *No, help me.*

And my rage builds. It seems so unfair.

————

People think prayer is something you do when you are alone.

When you address the God-who-lives-above or the God-who-lives-within, you do it privately. Solo. Even Jesus says you should go into your room and close the door to pray. And there is something to that.

Prayer is an extremely intimate act.

But I think the *most* intimate form of prayer is the prayer you address to God-as-God-lives-within-another.

And that is what is happening now.

Mom is asking me to speak for God and tell her what she needs to hear.

She is asking me to speak for God and give her a comforting word.

And God-who-lives-within-me would like to give it.

But he's got to deal with me first.

Mom is asking for permission to die a little bit today.

And I know what needs to be said and I bitterly resent it.

But I say it.

I say, *We're NOT GOING.*

And I say suddenly, angrily, firmly, and in a voice that admits of no discussion, *We're NOT going.*

I say it, almost shout it, as if I were defying somebody — who? myself, I suppose — I say, *We're NOT going.* It's the exact right thing to say, said in a wildly inappropriate way.

Then silence.

Neither of us moves.

Then Mom nods and I pick up the phone, call the doctor's office and, seemingly adult, cancel. The chief nurse, Chris, lovely as always, sends her love to Mom and will have somebody come from the lab to do Mom's blood work at home. I tell her that I will call later in the week to remake the appointment.

I hang up the phone and call Pat, who tells me *now* that it is *minus seven degrees.*

At Mom's request, I call Paulette and tell her we canceled. She says, *Well CERTAINLY. Only a FOOL would go out in this weather,* and that ends the episode.

————

Mom and I continue to sit at the kitchen table, silent. One problem is solved, but now there is another. Mom, as always, attacks it directly. Quietly, but directly.

Mom asks, *Are you mad at me, Billy?*

And, when there is no answer, she continues softly, *Don't be mad.*

Silence.

I tell her honestly that I am mad. That I don't know at what, but I don't think it's at her. Probably it's mostly that I am frustrated because I was trying so hard to get her up and out and, well, it wasn't to be.

She accepts that, though I don't know if I do.

I tell Mom I'm going out for a walk. I have to do something with all the accumulated momentum. Mom, relieved not to be going out, says that I should take the key because she's going to get undressed and lie down for a while.

———

The freezing cold feels invigorating to me.

I walk without any place to go in this suburban development. I yearn for a bookstore or a cafe where I could sit and gather my thoughts. But there is only a hardware store and a lumberyard and even they're not open yet.

So, I try to walk off my anger and my momentum …and I think of a story.

A story from Dad's childhood that I have always loved.

When he was a kid, there were still horse-drawn sleighs in the street and he used to hitch rides on the back of them. Once the horse took a sudden turn and the runners of the sleigh ran across both of his legs. He was so scared that his legs were broken that he ran all the way home to find out.

Momentum.

Dad's personal form of momentum was driving. He loved to drive. If you asked my father for a lift to the subway, he'd ask, *Where you going?* and after you'd told him, he'd say, *Forget the subway. I'll take you there.* And he would. On a summer night, he didn't even need to have a destination for a trip. *Kids, want to go for a ride? Hop in the car,* and we always would, leaving Mom to get some peace and quiet. *Can the Gomez kids come?*

*Sure.*

*And the McDonalds?*

*Hop in.*

And we were off.

*Where we going, Dad?*

*We're going for a RIDE!*

When Dad's momentum began to fail him, he did not rage against the dying of the light.

He tried chemotherapy for an afternoon, decided it wasn't for him, and then settled into the business of enjoying the six months Dr. McK had said he had left.

As soon after the surgery as he could, he went back to driving Mom to the store and church. Some months later, when his strength was running out, Mom came out of a store, found Dad slumped over the wheel, and thought, mistakenly, that he was dead. There was no complaint, no rage. He simply gave up driving, stayed home, and let the world come to him.

As Dad could move less and less, I had to carry him.

He would lock his fingers and put his arms around my neck so I could hoist him out of his big soft chair and then move him as you would move a large refrigerator box. Pivot a bit, pivot to the other side a bit and, bit by bit, we would make our way down the corridor. Dad, always the good dancer, called it waltzing. So, several times a day, I would waltz him to the bathroom and hold him up as he did his necessary bathroom tasks.

Then, one night while I was holding Dad up at the toilet, he suddenly let his hands drop and, for a long moment, he was pissing all over the walls and the floor, his urine splashing on our feet and legs. Since both of my hands were supporting him, I couldn't do much for the moment, but, from that time forward, I held my father's heavy, blunt penis whenever he had to urinate.

Dad was gracious and I was grateful to return some of the favors he had done for me over a lifetime. And, I suppose, in my twenties and anxious to be full-fledged as an adult, I flattered myself into thinking that a role reversal had taken place, that I had become the parent and he the child.

Chess.

As Dad spent more and more of his time just sitting, we would play, as we always had, endless games of chess.

I cheated in what I rightly assumed would be our last game. I intentionally made an attack on his king that left my queen undefended. I could sense his anticipation the moment he saw my gaffe, and, when I lifted my hand from the piece I was moving, Dad hooted with delight and stole my queen from the board. From then on, I played as hard as I could, knowing that with this advantage he would win the last game we ever played. I continue to enjoy that loss more than any victory I have ever won.

When chess became too strenuous, we just talked.

We had always just talked. Freely, easily, and about everything. From the time I was in late grammar school and all through high school, we stayed up late to talk, laugh, and tell stories. *For Christ sake, Pete,* Mom would shout from the bedroom, *the boy has to go to school in the morning!* But it would usually already be morning by that point and we would just keep talking. As we did as he was dying.

After a while, even conversation became too demanding.

Dad would ask me to read to him and I would read him to sleep at night, though Dad would not make it easy. He would not shut his eyes and this irritated me. I would be exhausted from taking care of him all day and here I was, a good guy, trying to comply with his wishes, and he wouldn't even cooperate with his own plan for going to sleep.

So, after reading for a while, I would look over to see if he had fallen asleep yet so that I could go to bed, and his eyes would be wide open. *Dad, shut your eyes or neither of us are going to get any sleep.* He would nod, shut his eyes peacefully, and settle into his pillows, and I would go back to reading again. When I looked over later, his eyes would be open again. *Daaaaaaaad*...Dad, caught, would laugh and quickly slam his eyes shut, which would make me smile. After more reading, I'd look again and, playfully, he had one eye closed and one eye open. I was tired but I laughed and barked, *CLOSE YOUR EYES!*

And he didn't.

He didn't joke about it anymore either.

He just kept looking at me.

I asked him, *Don't you want to sleep?*

Silence.

And then he said—*I just want to look at you, Billy.*

Silence.

*I just want to look at you, Billy.*

I realized he didn't want to hear the book. He wanted to see his son. That's all he wanted on the last nights of his life. So I returned to reading without further objection, without looking up to see if he was asleep. I let his gaze fall on me, like the sun.

And that is why, though there seemed to be so many role reversals late in Dad's life, I was never in any real way able to switch roles with him. Because, even though I was reading him to sleep, tucking him in, taking him to the bathroom, doing everything you would do for a child, he was never more my father than when, deprived of all ability to do any other father-like thing, he sat there and looked at me with utter wonder and unlimited approval. And in that, my father—able to do practically nothing—taught me perhaps the most important lesson of my life: what God is.

Half the time, I don't even know what God is. But I do, sometimes, experience a mystery—a vast and caring mystery —that gets past my defenses and into my soul and says I— even I—might matter. Vastly. That, limited as I am, I might be irreplaceable, unrepeatable, and of unlimited worth.

When that happens, that's called God.

*I just want to look at you, Billy.*

———

And when Dad's momentum was finally completely spent (and it carried him half-again as long as the doctor had predicted), Pete Cain, Mary's Pete, Paul and Billy's dad, finally went gently into that good night.

With flawless timing, my dad died on Father's Day.

———

As I walk in the minus-seven-degree cold, I think of Dylan Thomas and his famous advice.

When I give friends tours of my neighborhood in New York, I always stop at the place where the great poet died. Inevitably we quote his magnificent words, *Rage, rage against the dying of the light* . . .

But on this cold, bright morning, thinking now of the gentle beauty of my father's death, I find myself reevaluating my admiration for the poet and the poem. I find myself thinking, *When it comes to death, what the hell did Dylan Thomas know about it anyway?*

Dylan Thomas, utterly alone, drank himself to death over the course of a winter's night in a dirty bar on Eighth

Avenue South. His own death was pathetic, stupid, wasteful. Taking that into consideration, it suddenly seems very odd that anybody would take his advice about the meaning of death at all seriously. Rage? Why rage? Why not, as my father did, die with dignity, acceptance, and love? Why not do it consciously? Hand oneself over to death and, in so doing, offer gifts of love to those that remain behind. Why *not* go gently into that good night?

And I began to feel more accepting of Mom's dying. If not going to the doctor was a step toward a graceful leaving, so be it. Maybe that wasn't so bad. In any case, it has a lot more to recommend it than drinking yourself to death in the White Horse Tavern.

And, finally, freezing and somewhat more comfortable with the idea and presence of death, I went home.

———

Back in the apartment, I call out *I'm home* and there is no response.

The house is completely silent, which is odd, because, if Mom wasn't on the phone, the radio or the television was usually on.

I check around and find her on her bed in a deep sleep.

She had managed to only start changing clothes before she fell asleep, so she is still in her good clothes.

She is perfectly still ... except that her feet move a bit as they always do when she is having a dream. In her dreams, she walks. The momentum is still in there somewhere. And I find myself thinking, absurdly, *It's not that cold. Really, it's not. And you were already dressed. We could have made it.*

*We could have made it.*

*We really could have ...*

I think, *We could make it even now.*

*We'd be a little late, and I know how you hate that, but at least we could still show up...*

I stand there—a child—absurdly scared and absurdly mad, willing my mother to get up, and, in my own way, praying an utterly hopeless prayer from the deepest, quietest, stillest part of me, unmoving and alone.

*It's a beautiful day. Are you sure you want to sleep? There's so little time. We could be out. And if you don't want to go to the doctor's, that's all right too. It doesn't have to be to the doctor's. We could go anywhere. We could just, you know, go for a ride. Wouldn't you like to go for a RIDE?*

And, finally, against all reason, I think, *Don't sleep. Don't. No. Don't. Please wake up. Wake up and rage with me.*

*Rage, rage against the dying of the light...*

### Chapter 10. What Does Dylan Thomas Know About It Anyway?

When I think back on our tiny apartment, I can't remember many religious images, but the few that I can recall are vivid.

A crucifix on the wall of the living room that was a wedding present from the priest who had married my parents. Not a frightening one. Arms extended in protection.

Statues—maybe two or three, one that fascinated me as a child.

A small, wooden self-contained shrine, wonderfully carved. You could open the doors and there was St. Francis of Assisi waiting to greet you. I had a sense of awe about it.

But the real images of godliness and—even God—were much closer.

So close you could touch them.

I now look back in my imagination and memory to see where God actually was and am shaken by how much love was given to me. How closely I was watched, protected, fed, washed, clothed. How close was God? And I didn't know it.

I thought it was just my parents.

How close was God in your house?

## 11

# *Beyond the Five Stages*

---

Elizabeth Kübler-Ross taught the world that dying has five stages.

I believe almost everything has five stages.

I even believe that the five stages have five stages.

I know this because I am currently in the first stage of one of the stages. I am cranky—which I believe to be the first stage of the Anger Stage of dying.

Only I am not dying.

My mother is dying and she is happy as a clam watching the Winter Olympics. She is so cheerful she is pushing me into the second stage of anger—which is grumpy.

I am cranky because, days ago, I sent the script I have been working on for months to the project's producer. I am waiting to hear—today?—if the film will be green-lighted. While waiting, I would love to go out and wander around. Maybe buy the *New York Times*. And I could do this. The grocery store—not *that* far away—carries the *Times*. I could walk over and buy it—if we weren't in the middle of a blinding blizzard in the middle of a winter that is setting records for snow accumulation. Hence, I am cranky. *Billy, come on out. It's the speed skating finals for the 1000 meters. You'll love it!* No, I am not cranky. I am grumpy.

As a kid, I mastered the stages of anger.

I could go from 1. Cranky, to 2. Grumpy, to 3. Angry, to 4. Mad, to 5. Enraged *very* quickly. On a bad day, I could go all the way to full blow-out tantrum—which combines all five previous stages and transcends them. What's on the other side of the tantrum I don't know—I have never gotten there—but I expect jail-time is involved.

My parents, assuming I would outgrow tantrums (which I have...mostly), never interfered with them. They would watch, tsk-tsk, and wait till they ended, as they inevitably did, with me kicking a piece of furniture and collapsing to the floor, wailing, holding my stubbed toes, at which point my father, genuinely puzzled, would ask, *But, Billy, what does it get you?*

Dad, who was a good teacher, could never teach me to get past tantrums because he never understood them. Like the rest of us, he had a temper, but unlike the rest of us, he rarely went over the top—even when I, as a teenager, would off-handedly savage his most deeply held beliefs pretty much just for the hell of it. Dad, thinking he was fighting for my soul, rose to the bait every time and the two of us would go at it into the wee hours of the morning. Even so, I rarely saw him mad.

But it did happen.

I was fourteen and therefore utterly contemptuous when my father forbade me to read a book which he had heard (correctly) was blasphemous. He, of course, found where I hid the book, which I, of course, had bought and read. Dad, who read whatever my brother and I were reading—*The Once and Future King* and *The Godfather* were his favorites—read the blasphemous book in a sitting. When he finished it at one o'clock in the morning (I was up cramming for a test) he threw open my bedroom door and stood, filling the doorway and holding the book in his hand. He tossed the book on my bed and said, *very* quietly, *I want this book out of my house.*

I knew from what he *didn't* say that he was conceding my right to read whatever book I wanted as long as I didn't bring it home.

I said, *OK, Daddy*—a name I had not called him in years.

———

Annoyed by my mother's cheerfulness, I decide to walk the impassable roads up to the store to buy the paper.

In Kübler-Ross terms, this is denial.

I don't care.

Mom objects to my going out in such weather for something as silly as the paper.

I don't care.

I convince her with two magic words: dishwashing liquid. We're out of dishwashing liquid which, to my mother, constitutes a crisis, and I prepare to step into the blizzard. I dress warmly in so many layers that my arms, kid-like, won't hang at my sides and off I go.

———

Once out, I am winded quickly.

I've gotten no exercise while writing the script. In fact, toward the deadline, to keep my energy up, I had begun Hershey therapy. If I wasn't actually drinking Hershey syrup out of the can, I was very close.

I press on through the blinding snowstorm, my heart pounding wildly, until I realize I have absolutely no idea of where I am, other than in the middle of a white-out. Still, obsessed, I go on until it all gets just a little too Jack London for me and I am forced to retrace my vanishing steps back to the house, where Mom is watching biathletes successfully ski and shoot their way through a blizzard. *Isn't it just great, Billy?*

I go to my room and wait for the phone to ring, which it does not do for hours at a time.

I am now angry.

I tell myself that, if the snow stops, I will try again.

This is bargaining.

It works. Don't tell me it doesn't.

The storm stops, the sun comes out and it is stunningly, surrealistically clear.

I layer up and try again.

———

I step out the door and the insides of my nose and mouth freeze instantly.

They freeze hard.

This is sobering, but, obsessed, I tell myself that this life-threatening weather is, in fact, "brisk" and press on to the bottom of the first of three substantial hills I must climb. After taking a few steps on the first hill and finding myself exactly where I was before taking the steps, I realize why there are no cars out. Underneath the snow is pure ice. To get any footing at all, I have to slam my heel down hard, through the snow, into the ice. Even then, it's two steps forward/one step back, but—slam! slam! slam!—I am making progress.

By the top of the first hill, I am no longer cold. By the top of the second, I am sweating. By the top of the third, I want to lie down and take a nap in the snow.

But the strip mall is in sight.

To get there, I have to cross a main street and this is genuinely dangerous, since, should a car come down the hill, there would be no way it could stop for me. So, barely keeping my balance, I trot across the street and slide into the store. When I get there, I feel like planting a flag.

The store is open, but empty.

End-of-the-world empty.

No one is shopping; no one is at the registers.

Eventually, as I emerge from the cereal aisle, I startle the manager and a cashier, who, feet up, are sipping hot coffee in the deserted bakery, debating closing because *Who in their right mind would be out shopping today?*

I hesitate to agree.

When they ask how the driving is and I tell them that I walked, they ask, *What in hell could be so important that you walked all the way up here today?*

When I say *The New York Times*, there is a pause.

The cashier puts down her coffee, gets up, and goes to the front of the store, leaving the manager to tell me that *what with the weather and all* he didn't bother to pick up the papers because, well, he didn't expect anybody to be in. Then he smiles an open, friendly smile, expecting me to understand.

Silence.

He looks into my eyes and sees something that frightens him.

I am entering the fourth stage of anger.

I am mad.

Really mad.

After a moment of tense silence, the manager apologizes and then says, *But you have to admit, nobody in his right mind...*

He trails off.

I say, *That's alright,* in a tone that conveys just exactly how not alright it is, ask him where he keeps the dishwashing liquid, pick up a few other things that Mom needs, more Hershey syrup for me, and I walk to the front of the store where the cashier has already flipped the sign on the door from OPEN to CLOSED and has started to turn off the lights.

As I start back home, I discover that—Irish blessing notwithstanding—the wind at your back is no help at all when walking downhill on ice.

———

Downhill turns out to be much harder than up. I fall repeatedly before developing a workable technique: *very* small steps. Step step step step and I have covered a foot and a half. Step step step step—another foot and a half. Step step step and I think that step step step my arms sticking out and taking such tiny step step steps, I must look like a penguin step step who's been shopping step step step. Still, nobody's going to see me since nobody in their right mind would be out today—except maybe the guy who is driving what sounds like a very large car behind me. I can't actually see what it is until it comes over the ridge of the hill, but it is, in fact, not a car but a very large moving van.

STEPSTEPSTEPSTEPSTEPSTEPSTEP...

The van, grazing the snow banks on both sides of the road, is honking for me to get out of its way and I'd like to, but, if I run, I will definitely fall and I don't want to end up under that van. So, eyeing a driveway not that far away, I keep taking my penguin steps, but now as fast as I possibly can.

Stepstepstepstepstepstepstepstepstepstepstep...

As the van closes in on me, I think *What the hell!* and break into a full out run.

STRIDE! STRIDE! STRIDE! STRIDE! I take five or six huge steps (all pretty much in the exact same place) when my feet, after a brief back-wrenching struggle, disappear from under me. I fly into the air, and see, with that bizarre slo-mo vision that accompanies car accidents, my groceries flying happily upward all around me. The second I hit the ground—hard—I roll as fast as I can into the nearest driveway and listen as the van rumbles to a stop two houses before the house into whose driveway I have rolled.

As I lie on the ground without moving, a familiar feeling comes upon me. I recognize it as an old friend. On this cold, exhausting day, rage is welcome.

Rage is hot.

Rage is energetic.

Rage will get me up out of the snow bank.

Rage will bring me home.

When rage has filled my body completely, I rise, refuse help from the van party, and set about retrieving my scattered groceries. I pick them up one by one and put them in the bag. But something extremely odd, disturbingly odd, is happening. The groceries won't stay in the bag! As in a bad dream, no matter how often I put the groceries in the bag, they remain on the ground. In the bag. On the ground. In the bag. On the ground. In the...

It is only now that I realize exactly how mad I must be because it has taken me this long to notice the bag has an enormous hole it in. It is, in fact, no longer a bag, but a hole with handles. So I cram the groceries in my pockets and, I carefully work my way back to the apartment with tiny, tiny steps.

*Billy? Is that you? My, isn't it BEAUTIFUL out!*

Mom comes into the kitchen to help put away the groceries and asks innocently *Did you get...* but before she can finish her question I say, *Yes, I got the goddamn dishwashing liquid!* and slam it onto the table.

Seeing I am upset, and anxious to be of help, Mom asks what happened and I tell her. The snow. The ice. The cold. No *Times*. The walk. The van. The fall. The groceries-that-won't-stay-in-the-bag. EVERYTHING.

When I finish ranting, I feel much relieved...until I notice that my mother, my own mother, is smiling. No. Not smiling exactly. Not yet. But a small dolphin-like curl has appeared at the corner of her lip.

*WHAT? What's funny!!!*

She says, *Nothing,* but as she does, the dolphin-like curl leaps into a smile.

*WHAT? WHAT! WHAT'S FUNNY?*

*Well,* she says, *the bag broke?*

Now, when she started this very short sentence she was full of concern, *Well,* but by the time she got to *broke* she was clearly, openly amused.

This was a mistake.

I, with no sense of humor at all, say, *Don't. Don't you dare,* and she says, seriously, *I won't,* and—for a second—she doesn't. And then she does. She laughs. I say, *WHAT? WHAT!!!* And she says, smiling more broadly now, *Well, don't you see? After all that, the bag broke...* and she laughs full out.

I stand quietly for a moment. And then I blow.

Tantrum-time.

I SHOUT. I RAGE. I CURSE. I curse SYRACUSE, the WINTER, the MOVING VAN and THE GOD WHO WOULD PERMIT SUCH SUFFERING AS MINE, and finally I announce that I am GOING TO MY ROOM and I'm GOING TO BED and that I have NO intention WHAT-SO-EVER of GETTING UP till AAAAPRILLLLL!!!!

She thinks this is pretty funny too.

As I drift into a depressed sleep, I can hear Mom shuffling around in the kitchen, putting away the groceries and tsk-tsk-tsking...

———

When I wake, I can hear Mom cheering the Olympics.

It is dark.

I have slept longer than I intended and I feel post-tantrum hungover.

When I come into the living room, Mom is cordial to me, always a bad sign. She presents me with a pile of phone messages, the message from David Manson, the producer of the movie I have been waiting to hear about, on top.

Though sleepy and slightly punch-drunk from the events of the day, I decide to return the call. I ask Mom, somewhat grandly, to please turn down the television as I have a very important call to make.

She goes me one better, turns it off completely, walks over to the window, and looks out at the snow.

A bit tense, I dial David, the producer.

Now David is extremely smart, a bit reserved, and prone to saying things like, *It's a good beginning*, about scripts that I think are done and polished.

From sunny California, he answers.

But David doesn't immediately plunge into a discussion of the script as he usually would. He is friendlier, less professional than usual. Overeager, I take this as a sign that he liked the script even though he seems to be avoiding discussing it. He chats. So, fine, we chat and, after a while, he says, most pleasantly, *You know, Bill, I wasn't expecting to hear from you today.*

Since I answer David's calls promptly, I find this strange and tell him so.

He says *Yes, yes, of course, but I wasn't expecting to hear from you TODAY.* Puzzled, I ask, *Why not?*

I can hear a smile coming into his voice as he answers *Well, it was MY understanding—and I have this on VERY good authority —and I can hear the smile growing—that you were GOING TO YOUR ROOM and you were GOING TO BED and that you had NO intention WHAT-SO-EVER of GETTING UP till APRIL!*

I am stunned.

Silence.

He laughs.

I say nothing.

His impression of my tantrum is so exact that I wonder for a moment if—somehow—could our phone have been off the hook while I was blowing up and he had overheard me?

Then another possibility occurs to me.

I look into the living room where my mother stands, looking out at the snow, pretending not to be completely

delighted with herself.

I am speechless.

As professional, reserved David continues to chuckle, I wonder: What should I do?

I can feel myself moving beyond tantrum.

I decide, given the circumstances—the snow, the cabin fever, the events of the day—no jury in the world would go higher than manslaughter.

Then, something odd happens.

And I realize what is on the other side of the tantrum.

And it is *not* acceptance.

I fight it.

I fight it with everything within me.

Then, much, much, MUCH against my will, I feel a small dolphin-like curl start to form at the corner of my lip.

## Chapter 11. Beyond the Five Stages

Jorge: *Christ never laughed.*
William: *Can we be so sure?*
Jorge: *There is nothing in the Scriptures to say that He did.*
William: *And there's nothing there to say that He did not.*
                              —The Name of the Rose

Sarah laughed and Jesus wept.

Surely there must have been times when that reversed.

Sarah had many occasions for tears, not the least of which was the near-sacrifice of Isaac.

Was there laughter for Jesus?

The unexpected wine at Cana? Zacchaeus in the tree? Blind eyes opening? The miraculous catch of fish? The absurdity of it all?

In most cases, he found his way to a happy ending in his storytelling.

A man digging in a field finds a pearl. A drunken son, when all is lost, finds his way home to a loving father. A brutal robbery becomes the story of a healing.

And the sweep of his life shows that tragedy does not have the final say.

Is there a stage, in the life of Jesus, that goes beyond the five stages to arrive at joy?

Do we—sometimes—arrive at that stage?

## 12

# *The Lost Epistle of Paul*

If the Bible feels familiar to you, it should.

It is your story.

Even if you haven't read it, you've lived it.

You were born a new Adam or a new Eve and, if creation wasn't exactly new when you arrived, it was new to
you. Like Adam and Eve (and all the Adams and Eves
since), you beget your begats, fight your fights, say your
prayers and finally go to sleep. You take your journey
... and the world is saved or lost in you.

———

There was a certain inevitability to the journeys my brother
and I took.

Since medieval times, there have been accepted paths
for sons of parents with no land to leave them and we followed those paths: the younger, I went into the church to
become a priest, and Paul, the older, went to the military to
become a warrior

———

Alaska, 6 May, Sunday

Dear Mom & Dad,

Spring has sprung. I sat out in the sun today for about four hours working and it was great. I just don't think anybody has appreciated the sun until they have spent a winter in Alaska!

I still haven't received any orders so I'll be waiting again this week. The lack of orders is keeping me guessing, but I think I'm going to Vietnam. If this turns out to be true, you really won't have to worry. I will have a job as either a Fire Spt Coordinator at Bn or Bde level HQ or Fire Direction officer in the Bn HQ—either way, I'll be in a well-protected area!

When I do get orders, I'll probably get 30 days leave so I'll be home for an extended visit. Well, I have to write Bill tonight so I'll sign off now and write again soon.

Love, Paul

P.S. Please send another can of tobacco.

———

The greatest support you can have for your journey is the unconditional love of your family.

Except for two things:

The journey is always a journey away from your family's expectations and therefore accomplished only against their wishes and over their objections.

And, second...

Unconditional love ultimately imposes the harshest conditions of all.

Oklahoma, 16 June, Sunday

Happy Father's Day, Dad!

Ft. Sill is hot and very, very busy! I have been going every minute since I got here. It's been a wealth of information.

To tell you the truth, Dad, I'm not really overjoyed at going to a combat zone but it really doesn't worry me! Things couldn't be better to go really—besides a year & a half of good experience in a line unit I am getting the most comprehensive course possible in VC tactics, Air mobility, booby traps, Arty tactics and fire direction procedures...

By the way, I'm due to make Capt. the day I arrive in Vietnam. How about that, me a Cpt and getting up in the world?

A little info that will please Mom—if I can't leave here until 16 July I'm going to sell the car & fly home so I don't have to waste time driving. I can't wait to get to good old NYC and see everyone again!! I hope we can arrange to get to go up and see Bill while I'm home and a couple of days visiting in Syracuse might be interesting—after all Kathy must have some friends.

Well, I have to iron a uniform for tomorrow—see "y'all" soon—

Happy Father's Day, Dad, and hang in there— we're all going to get together shortly.

Your loving (but wandering) son,
Paul

————

In any family with two sons—Cain and Abel, Jacob and Esau, Paul and Billy—part of the family myth is always that one son is favored....

(Actually, the undergirding myth of our family was Dad's personal motto: *All things work together unto the good.* Still...)

Family myth has it that I was the favored child and Paul the less loved, and there is some truth to this. Paul came out of his childhood exhausted by his parents' demands; I came out of mine feeling completely accepted. This was *not*, however, because I got the lion's share of love. On the contrary, this was because, besides having been loved just fine, I was substantially ignored and this is a very great blessing for a child.

As I was the second child, my parents frequently took me for granted. If I failed at something or screwed up, they didn't rush to straighten me out or improve me. If I got into or caused trouble, their response was always the same. *Pete?* Mom would say to Dad...or Dad to Mom, *Mary? ...Are you sure we got the right baby at the hospital?*

My brother, on the other hand, was loved with a passion and it nearly killed him.

———

### Mother's Notes
Paul Francis born with black hair
(bald on top and plenty of black hair on sides and back of head)

In my continuing archeology of the family closets, I have come across a document called "Mother's Notes" that makes it clear just how completely my brother was loved.

His every action was noticed and carefully noted (in Mom's best handwriting) with the kind of attention usually reserved for infant Chinese emperors. Better than fifty years after the fact, for example, I can tell you that on...

> Nov 23rd – he laughed out loud
> for the first time.

...and that on...

> Dec. 30th – he held little red teddy bear in hands
> for first time.

...and on...

> Dec 31st – he started taking vegetables–
> started with spinach and it did not agree with him
> so started with carrots on Jan 5th seems to like
> these.

...and on...

> Jan 1st – started blowing bubbles – beginning to sit
> up and notice things around

There are no notes on the first time I threw up spinach or anything else. (My brother threw up prunes in early January.) There are no copies of my baby formula. (Paul's was 28 oz. milk, 4 oz. water, 4 tbsp. Dextra Maltese) or the times of my feedings (his were 7 a.m., 11 a.m., 2:30 p.m., and 6 p.m.).

My brother wasn't given gold, frankincense, and myrrh for his first Christmas, but I can tell what he was given. And who gave it. Mrs. Helen Rafferty of 617 Oakwood Ave. gave him a comforter; his first dollar came from Frank Leahy; Miss Sadie Kinney (who ran the bakery down the block) and Mrs. F. A. O'Connell went in together to get him a sweater. Etc., etc., etc.... The red teddy bear, mentioned above, was from Dad.

The only notes—make that "note"—I can find detailing my birth is scribbled, in pencil, in neither of my parents' handwriting, on the back of a list of babies with whom I shared Nursery 4. Evidently there were fourteen of us there at the time, including Baby Iacifano, Baby Duffy, Baby Martin, etc. The note about me says, in full:

**Baby Cain**
Birth weight      5.7
Present weight   5.9
Length             18 inches

On the note, somebody has scribbled a further note to give somebody else (illegible, and by now, probably dead) 25 mg. of C-vitamin or ascorbic acid—one tablet daily. That is the full surviving documentation of my infanthood. Not a very careful record. Who knows? Maybe there is reason to believe that they actually *did* get the wrong baby at the hospital.

And by the way, when I was brought home from the hospital, my brother tried to murder me in my crib. To this day he maintains that he was just trying to cut the ribbons off my bassinette so he could see me. Still, baby Paul, age three, temporarily dethroned emperor of 47-05 47th Avenue, Apt. 2F, Woodside, Queens, was found standing over his infant brother's crib with a sharp pair of scissors. You be the judge.)

I will spare you further details of my brother's infancy (*bowel movements seem good, but very dark brown*), but, if there was ever a doubt in my mind that the family myth was wrong, these notes have put it to rest.

The problem was not that my brother was *less* loved; the problem was that my brother was *too* loved.

———

I should tell you there was always an element of fear in my parents' love of Paul.

In the first place, they almost didn't have him; he came along only after six years of trying.... And the birth was so long and difficult that Dad's dad, Pop Cain, was afraid that both mother and child were lost.... And they actually *did* lose him once at Aunt Marg's summer camp on Otisco Lake....

The story was so rarely told, I'm not even sure Paul knows it.

Aunt Marg's camp stands on a substantial bluff—a cliff, really—and Paul, not much more than a toddler, fell off the edge and screamed for help. But when Mom and Dad and the uncles and aunts, terrified, ran to the shore below to rescue him, Paul was not there. They could hear him screaming for help, but he was nowhere to be seen. They couldn't find him and they were terrified.

(They lost me twice—at Macy's and at Jones Beach—but they never panicked. *Oh, Billy will turn up.* And, it seems, I did.)

Paul had disappeared.

Whether this lasted five seconds, five minutes, or five hours I never asked, but in the telling of the story—even years later—you could still hear the intensity of both the fear and the love.

Actually, on the way down the cliff, Paul had gotten snagged by a very small bush, which completely hid him. The acoustics of the cliff and the lake played games with Paul's desperate cries, so there he was, suspended in midair, screaming for help and there they were, consumed with fear and love, shouting "Where are you, Paul?" —looking right at him and not seeing him.

Fear + love = awe and awe was always part of the equation between my parents and their firstborn son.

———

Concluding Mother's Note:

Paul Francis' first Christmas —
He stared at lights on tree when lighted....

———

Speaking of Christmas, I think the baby Jesus and my brother Paul might have had similar problems.

Had Jesus been loved a little less, had Mary not written down all the gifts and visits at his birth, had expectations not been quite so high, he might have led a long, happy life and died in his bed surrounded by grandchildren.

Oh, the unintentional consequences of unconditional love...

———

Over the Pacific, 12 August

Dear Mom & Dad,
Things are AOK! I'm about 2 hrs out of RVN over the Pacific. Boy, it's a big ocean. By the way, chalk up

another state—we landed in Hawaii for fuel so I've been there too. This whole part of the ocean is dotted with small islands and most of them don't rise over 100' above sea level—I don't think I'd want to live in this part of the world!

Well, right now it is Sun 11 Aug, 9:05 PM Eastern Standard Time. In Vietnam it is 9:05 Mon 12 Aug so you figure it out!

I'll drop you another line soon—the return address on this is where you can write to me.

Love,
Paul

————

And, I admit it, I adored him too.

We fought—all kids do—but I thought he was a miracle.

He had a three-year head start on me, so, by the time I arrived, it seemed to me he already knew everything worth knowing.

More than that, he was kind to me. He let me ride on the back of his two-wheeler once he got one. And *never* that I can remember (and this astonishes me even now) never *once* when his friends were around—the demigods (to a younger brother) who made up the PAL baseball team— *never once* did he tell me to get lost.

What more could you ask for in a brother?

I thought he was perfect.

So did my parents...and that was a problem.

————

Because they saw his potential (infinite) so clearly, it seemed to me that my parents frequently didn't see *him* ... or how hard he was trying (very). Nobody ever tried harder than my brother. *When Paul was a little boy g*oes one of the stories ...

*When he was just a little boy, we were sitting at a soda foun- tain getting ready to order and he drank his glass of water. The waitress saw the glass was empty, so she filled it. Paul emptied the glass again. So the waitress filled it again and he drank it again. So the waitress filled it again. And he drank it again. And again. And again ... until finally he said,* Mommy, make her stop. I can't *drink* any more. ... *That's just how he was.* ...

———

From the start, my brother was perfectly willing to drink the cup to the dregs.

Having been greatly loved, Paul became great-hearted and would give his great heart to whatever was asked of him. Where I was skeptical of, for example, that peculiar blend of bogus-Indian-lore and militia-activity that is the Boy Scouts, Paul leapt in, earned his merit badges and be- came a Life Scout. *Paul, want to be an altar boy?* Introibo ad altare Dei. *Want to run track?* Captain of the team. Paul would do anything. ...

Except study.

He wouldn't study—I don't know why, he was bright enough—but he wouldn't, and this was the cause of endless fights in the house ... many of them spectacular. The folks put so much pressure on Paul sometimes it would make me cry. I thought the family was coming apart. Paul, not above trying to exploit my tears, would say, *Tell them why you're crying! Maybe it will help!* It never did. And who knows?

Maybe all the fights were necessary. Even as a kid, you have to separate yourself from your parents *somehow* (Jesus ran away from home at thirteen) and Paul drew the line at school. He would *not* be smart.

In fact, according to the report cards I've found, Paul did just fine at school, but just *fine* wasn't enough. *Fine* was a cause for war.

In any field other than school, he was exemplary.

––––––––

Paul was, as his Boy Scout oath required, honest, cheerful, thrifty, courteous, kind, brave, clean and reverent, intent on doing his duty to God and his country—dangerous things to ask so casually of a kid as pure in his striving as my brother. Witness the oldest piece of Paul's writing I can find, a handwritten rough draft of a high school letter to his congressman:

> Dear Senator Keating,
>
> Since entering ~~Xavier~~ St. Francis Xavier Military High School I have ~~believed~~ desired to attend the United States Military Academy at West Point, New York. The reason for this is I believe ~~this is~~ my vocation ~~in life~~ is a career in the United States Army. I also know I can make myself a credit to my school and my country.
>
> Thanking you for a chance to prove myself, I am
>
> Respectfully yours,
>
> Paul Cain.

Personally, I think Paul joined the service simply because it was the hardest thing anybody asked him to do.

––––––––

In any case, Paul, highly motivated, went to a Jesuit military high school.

I, insane, followed him there. I didn't know where else to go. Besides, at least for my freshman/his senior year, I could take the subway with him into Manhattan in the mornings. This is a *bad* reason to go to a military school and, of course, it eventually backfired.

When West Point rejected Paul, he went to college, took ROTC, went through OCS and ended up in the same place anyway.

14 Aug, Wed, Vietnam

Dear Mom & Dad,

Well, today I got my assignment to the 1 Bn 5 Arty in Quan Loi. Right now I'm in Phu Loy at Div Arty HQ but I landed at Bien Hoa and was shipped to a Repo Depo at Long Binh. Now have you got all of that? If not I'll start again....

During his year-long tour of duty in the Republic of Vietnam, my brother wrote home once a week. And, as I explore the apartment's closets, I have found every letter and every envelope. They were saved and kept in strict chronological order.

Amazingly, during his August-to-August stay, he missed writing home only one week completely.

———

... It was a long flight (18 hrs) but as we flew over the coastline of Vietnam you wouldn't believe the sight. The fleet was steaming South along the coast and there must have been 30 ships of all sizes and

shapes. It made you feel good, knowing that there
are some friends around....

*It made you feel good, knowing that there are some friends around....*
I have read Paul's letters home many times since uncovering them, but I didn't make it through them the first time I tried.
Or the second.
Or third.
I found them frightening.
But the first time I tried to read them, it wasn't fear that stopped me. It was simple embarrassment at seeing how I was reflected in the letters. Or, more accurately, not reflected...

It's Bill's birthday tomorrow and I'm going to write
him as soon as I finish this. By the way, tell that little
pipsqueak of a brother that I haven't heard from him
at all yet...

Sometimes Paul is patient with me; sometimes not. He writes gently—

When you talk to Bill next tell him to drop me a
line. I have written him a couple of times since
his last letter—besides he is an excellent letter
writer...

And not so gently—

The next time you talk to that so-and-so tell him if
he doesn't write soon I'm going to skin him alive
when I get back....

Either way, when he finally gives up on me *(P.S. Tell Bill I still haven't heard from him but it's good to know he's doing well)*, it's quite a relief.

The reasons I wasn't writing are reflected in the letters (also saved) that I was writing home at the time...mine from the Novitiate of St. Andrew's which I had entered to begin a ten- to fifteen-year course of study to become a Jesuit priest.

———

Both my brother and I were pursuing ancient professions, but I had actually stumbled into the Middle Ages. When I entered St. Andrew's, people there were still speaking Latin. In cloistered, rural seclusion, we chanted Latin hymns, meditated till we had calluses on our knees and wore long black robes that made us look like contemporaries of the saints in the statues all around us. We were being brilliantly prepared to live the life of priests in the fifteenth century.

Then, the year after I entered—

## Vatican OKs Modernization
## Of Training for Priests

*(As Mom saved our letters, Dad clipped and saved newspaper articles about anything that might affect his sons' journeys through the world....)*

Vatican City (AP) Calling for experimentation on a "vast scale," the Vatican opened the door yesterday to psychoanalysis and other methods to help modernize training for priests, nuns and lay brothers in Roman Catholic religious communities...

The Second Vatican Council had said that, rather than relying so heavily on tradition, we had to look for God in the modern world...which was fine by me. But, as all the chanting, robes, and accompanying mystique disappeared, seminaries emptied. By the time the dust settled, not much more was left of our elaborate training program than a rough-and-tumble, no-holds-barred scavenger hunt for God...which is not a bad description of religious life at its essence.

———

Dad's clippings about the Second Vatican Council were kept right next to his clippings about the war.

Some of the clippings are general...*Enemy Fires Rockets Into Danang Killing 11 Civilians*...but most are about specific young men from our neighborhood. I suppose Dad studied the papers every day hoping *not* to see his son's name there among the other local kids who were bit by bit filling up Woodside's Calvary Cemetery.

### College Champ Dies in Vietnam

The Defense Department reported yesterday that a Marine from Maspeth had been killed in Vietnam bring the total number of war dead from Long Island to 638. Lance Cpl. Thomas P. Noonan, Jr....was the metropolitan area collegiate heavyweight wrestling champion the year he graduated from Hunter College in Manhattan....

And this explains a bit why I was not writing to my brother while he was in Vietnam.

## GI Killed on Eve of Birthday;
## Major Dies in Viet Action

Two more Long Island soldiers have been killed in Vietnam, bringing to 641 the number of Long Islanders killed in the war... SP/4 Robert T. Hamilton, 20, died last Tuesday, the day before his 21st birthday, when he stepped on an enemy booby trap. . . .

What could I—who was spending a great deal of my time in the streets protesting the war—say to my brother who was risking his life fighting it?

————

And, I suppose, I was afraid of what he would say to me.

I don't mean what he would say about my protesting. I knew that would be alright with him. You could always say whatever you wanted in our house.

But knowing how completely my brother gave himself to his commitments, I was afraid of what he would say about the war—afraid of exactly what I *did* find as I got deeper into his letters. And this is what caused me to stop reading Paul's letters for the second time.

Sat 24 August

Dear Mom & Dad,

I'm the Fire Spt Coordinator for the 1/26 Inf and have been very busy! We have run into fire fights 3 times since I have been here and my job is to put accurate, continuous, close Arty fire on the enemy without endangering friendly troops. So far my Arty has been credited with killing 14 gooks. That is the slang name for NVA (North Vietnamese Army). We have a real fine Battalion here and I'm not really worried at all. You see, I have a Bn of Infantry and 4 Arty Btrys around here so I feel very adequately protected.

The only thing that gets a little nerve racking is the waiting. This is about 80% to 90% planning and 10% to 15% fighting but both actually keep me pretty busy.

So far, so good, except it is extremely hot and humid around here and this makes sleeping very difficult. In order to give you an idea of where I am— I'm in War Zone D about 25 miles NE of Bien Hoa and the most recent fight we were in was at Tay Nin. We fired close to 400 rounds into that area and I understand the body count was 1 US KIA vs 476 NVA KIA (KIA is Killed In Action). I guess we really are winning.

Well, back to work. I'll write again soon.

Love,
Paul

PS. I'm now a fightin' CAPT!
Paul

And, who knows? Maybe I was jealous, too. As my rituals were disappearing around me, Paul was being welcomed into the community of warriors in rituals as old as religion, maybe older—

———

Mon 14 Oct

Dear Mom & Dad,

Well, last night we extracted from War Zone D and our three day patrol and this morning we are loading up for a 4 day operation—we are going to land 500 meters from the Cambodian Border and our mission is to look for the 165th NVA Regiment of the 7th NVA Division. I hope we don't find them! And yet I hope we do—someone has to finish this blasted war!

Well, folks, I have been on this operation for 4 days and you would disown me if you ever saw me! I have crawled under bamboo, waded in waist deep streams, hid in B-52 Bomb craters and slept out in the open with no cover—yes, it is quite a war. You would never believe it! By the way, I'm down to a mere 145 lbs—better watch out dad, I'll be ready to take you on. In Frisco on 9 Aug. Are you ready?

Well, I just received Dad's letter and I'm sitting in an RON/AP site (Rest overnight/ambush patrol) on the same operation. Tomorrow we get extracted (lifted out by 'chopper) and return to base camp at Quan Loi! From there we'll probably get a day's rest and then out on another operation!

I'm an Arty LNO (Liaison Officer) that is the Arty representative anywhere they go I go too—my job is to get all the Arty that Bn CO wants and sometimes it's not easy—but I like it—I'm a real part of this outfit and they are a proud unit—the 1st BN 26 INF (they call themselves the Blue Spaders and have quite a ceremony). In order to be a "Blue Spader" you have to be in a firefight with them, walk and/or crawl 10 miles in one day and drink a "Blue Blazer" after saying "Once a Blue Blazer, always a Blue Blazer, once a Blue Spader, always a Blue Spader." A Blue Blazer is a shot glass of Dramboui which they light (yes, with a match) and once lit you hold the glass high and sing out that saying and then down it. Of course these things come at Base Camp which we see about twice a month. Don't worry I haven't got a scratch on me and I've already gone through the initiation....

In the next letters, one a week, there are anniversary wishes to the folks, weather reports, military movements...

22 Oct – We are now working out of Long Me-Sihon near what is called the "Fishhook," 5 kilometers from Cambodia, but nothing much is happening. I guess the VC/NVA just don't want to fight prior to the elections because when we do find some, they shoot a couple of rounds then high tail it back north towards Cambodia!

...and...

30 Oct – Wed – Happy Halloween – Surprise! I remembered Bill's birthday tomorrow and I'm going to write him as soon as I finish this. By the way, tell that little pipsqueak of a brother that I haven't heard from him at all yet.
    Well, I'll see you in nine months.

Love,
Paul

Then, no letter the next week.

A week of silence.

It is at this point that my brother's letters become truly frightening.

---

I don't know how long it took for my parents to figure out that Paul's letters after the-week-with-no-letter were, if not exactly lies, intentionally misleading.

---

I am sure they saw it before I did. After all, I was reading the letters as a complete set, knowing that there would, in fact, be a full year's worth of them. They had to wait a week for each letter as it arrived like light from a star whose continued existence is in doubt. They had a week to ponder and pull apart each letter, so I'm sure they saw the contradictions before I did. Even then, it must have taken time because each individual letter is resolutely upbeat....

Every week, my brother assured his parents that he was fine.

Every week he was thankful for the brownies, reported on the weather, asked for simple things, acknowledged their arrival, sent presents, and, above all, told his parents *DON'T WORRY. If I know you at all, you're spending half your time worrying—STOP! Now! I have no problems and I'm in as safe a job as one can have in a war—so stop worrying now!* So it's not any single letter that gives Paul away; it's the contradictions as the letters mount up.

One letter will say *things are better now,* but there was never a prior letter saying anything was bad to begin with. Another will say *I don't worry anymore. I know I can do the job* when all previous letters had said he was never worried at all. A letter will say *The situation here has quieted down a bit* after saying for weeks that things were dull. Or that he just got out of the hospital because last week *the Bn Doc seemed to think I had malaria* when all he had said the week before was, *If you get a chance, how about sending over O. Henry, Shakespeare and Advanced Calculus? With these I would have a complete life.* Or, almost bizarrely—

Sun, 2 Feb –

Dear Mom & Dad,

This will have to be a short note—again there is no change here. All quiet these days in our area— hope it stays that way. I was awarded a Bronze Star yesterday—I'll send it home as soon as I get a chance to get to the post office....

There is no explanation for the Bronze Star. Just *The Polaroid pictures I received of you today had nobody smiling. Come on, we have more to be happy and thankful about than our share. Just promise me you won't worry about me as I have a nice safe job now and there is no sweat! OK?*

No, not OK. *Everything's fine; I just got the Bronze Star* makes no sense and I'm sure Mom and Dad sat at the kitchen table and talked this over. And over...

On rare occasions you can get a glimpse of what Paul is actually feeling, but only in a backhanded way. Writing about one his friends from the PAL baseball team, Paul says, *Tom always was a good guy. I'm glad he didn't get orders here.* Or, more tellingly, about another family friend, *Mike was lucky. If he's wounded as badly as you say he probably won't see this place for a long time....*

But after the missing letter in late October/early November, you have to read my brother's letters for what they *don't* say.

———

After the missing letter, there are no more gooks.
After the missing letter, there are no more KIA's.
There are no more body counts.
Rarely is anyone even hurt—on either side.
After the missing letter, nobody dies in my brother's war.

———

Dad must have known what was going on.

He followed the war on a map tacked up in our old bedroom and he occasionally forces Paul to be marginally more forthcoming. *You're right in one respect,* Paul will admit, *I have seen my share of action... or... I guess by now you've read about Sunday 11 May being the start of the summer offensive...* but Paul *offers* nothing, illuminates nothing. This must have been hard on Dad, to whom Paul had written a year earlier *It really is wonderful to be able to talk to your family on anything that may happen....*

Slowly, cheerfully, week by week, Paul becomes so hidden, so completely a stranger that, by the time he arrives back in Woodside to see Dad's WELCOME HOME, PAUL sign hanging from the fire escape, my brother will frighten his father and terrify his mother.

But even without Paul telling him, I am sure Dad knew what was going on the week-with-no-letter. It is the *only* week for which Dad saved multiple clippings from several newspapers. This is the *New York Times* article he saved from that week:

## U.S. BASE REPELS A MAJOR THRUST,
## FIRST IN A MONTH

―――

### *About 500 of Enemy Attack*
### *Near Cambodian Border*
### *Breaking Lull in War*

An enemy assault force charged an American position today, the first such attack in a month, but was turned back after hours of bitter fighting.

The major enemy thrust towards Julie, a nearby support base which lies 50 miles north of Saigon and only two miles from the Cambodian border came down at 3 A.M. and lasted until dawn....

### *Five Defenders Killed*
An officer said that of the 400 men in the camp when it was attacked, 5 were killed and 17 wounded.

"This is very fruitful for us," said Major Leonard Phillips, a brigade staff officer with the First Infantry Division. "We hope they will attack our night defensive positions. That way we don't have to go out and look for them...."

Dad must have noticed that the story is posted from Quan Loi, South Vietnam (Oct. 26). Dad, with his map, must have known that (from the day Paul arrived, *Today I got my assignment to the 1 Bn 5 Arty in Quan Loi* to the previous week's *I am waiting for a chopper to Quan Loi near the Cambodian Border)* Quan Loi was all over Paul's letters.

―――

Paul did not save letters from home, but one letter from Mom survives.

As is typical of her, determined to find out what's going on, she writes him a list of direct questions on a sheet of lined yellow pad. She asks, *Dear Paul: Questions? Just answer on this sheet and mail it in your letter, Paul. Thanks a million. Love—Mom. Where are you? Are you located in the Lai Khe (we think it is northwest of Saigon on the map)?*

They can't find him.

Paul answers:

Yes, it is about 18 miles NW of Saigon—but it is a full day's drive to Saigon and back—if you don't get ambushed! HA! HA!

They were losing him and they knew it.

Whatever he was becoming, he was becoming on his own.

———

Reading Paul's letters, I begin to understand why people stopped adding books to the Bible.

Most of the final books of the New Testament are made up of letters.

The stories in which God freely walked the earth—Creation, Adam and Eve, Cain and Abel, Noah's Flood—had already been written. They had yielded to the dawn-of-human-memory journeys of Abraham and Sarah in which God, though less seen, still drops by on occasion to dine. By the time Moses and David are engaging in the political struggles of their day, God is still seen, but only as a miraculously burning bush or a pillar of fire, and his words are now consigned to the thunder of the great prophets—Isaiah, Jeremiah, Ezekiel. . . .

They, in their turn, lead us into the comparatively modern times of the Roman Empire in which Jesus's story is told four times over, as if trying to find meaning in so simple a story of so simple a carpenter. Now, as even the pillars of fire and burning bushes disappear and the Red Sea no longer magically opens, we are left with nothing but carpenters and fishermen. Of course there are still miracles, but the Gospel doesn't rely on them for plot as the Pentateuch does (in fact, the Gospels work perfectly well without them) and the story becomes profoundly—almost exclusively— human....

And, as the writing of the Bible finally catches up with the events of daily life, history overtakes myth completely and holy writ, scripture, divine revelation becomes nothing more than a series of letters people are sending one another. Letters to the Romans, to the Corinthians, the Galatians...

Just letters—bringing one another up to date on news, sending love, quarrelling, taking sides in controversies, ask-ing for money—ordinary letters from ordinary people struggling to figure out who they are....

I think it was the letters that scared the people in charge of the Bible.

Don't we all get them? Send them?

Could this simple, intimate, fallible stuff really be the revelation taking us deeper into the unspeakable mystery of God?

Oh, St. Paul could still let loose with a sentence that thundered with prophetic certainty. *"For freedom are we set free!"* or my father's motto *"All things work together unto the good!"* But most often, St. Paul is just one of us trying to work out the endless contradictions of his own very compli-cated life. *I cannot understand my own behavior* he says.

> *I cannot understand my own behavior!* I fail to carry
> out the things I *want* to do and find myself doing
> the *very* things I *hate!*... *Instead* of doing the good

things I *want* to do, I carry out the sinful things I do
*not* want. In fact this seems to be the *rule*! *Every—
single—time* I want to do something *good,* something *evil* comes to hand! What a wretched man I
am! Who will rescue me from this body of
death?...

It is frightening to watch St. Paul tear his soul apart trying to express the new thing that he is becoming even
though the words for it did not yet exist. Still, he keeps on
writing because he can't stop believing that *glory shall be revealed in us!* He strains—as every word in the Bible has since
Abraham didn't kill Isaac—to contain the vast rage of divine passion within the limits of human tenderness. When
St. Paul finally manages to combine ancient contradictions
to create new truth, it will be contained not in a new Genesis or a new gospel, but in a few brave, searching letters to
friends.

I think St. Paul's half-crazed, soul-searching letters
scared the Bible-makers. But they weren't scared that God
had *stopped* speaking. They were scared that God was *still*
speaking—in the complexity of their own hearts and the
hearts of the people they knew. What if divine revelation
were that close? That deeply embedded in their own hu-
manity? Of course they were scared....

Scared like I was scared reading my brother's letters.

Scared by the amount of darkness he was containing
and not passing on. Scared at the depth of his loneliness as
he struggled to do something harder than the hardest thing
ever asked of him. Scared by the power of the transformation I could feel going on under his words, a transformation
that Dag Hammarskjöld describes well in the silence of his
own secret journals saying that *heat, denied any outlet,
changes coal into diamonds....*

I think people got scared of what would be required of them if *their* letters were to be revelations of God, so they decided that the font of revelation was closed.

But it wasn't closed.

On the contrary.

It was just close.

So close as to be frightening, maybe more frightening than a burning bush or a pillar of fire. For the journey that we all take—Abraham, Isaac, Jacob, Moses, David, which even God had to take—is to become who we are. *I am who am* God says, but only after years in the same desert where Jesus wandered and fasted and prayed, emerging to proclaim, with confidence, with authority, that he had found the Kingdom and found it close...so close that he had found it, in fact, within....

———

Once my brother becomes silent, there is no telling what he is going to become...except himself...and that, it seems to me, is the nature of every journey of the Bible.

The medieval monastic book *The Imitation of Christ* has been enormously popular for centuries, but it is, I think, a lie. *No one* in the Bible is an imitation of anyone else. Jesus is not an imitation of Moses. Moses is no copy of Abraham. They all take their journeys, and their journeys, like mine and yours, are uncharted and frightening because no one has been you before and somehow, and I don't know why, but somehow, each of us, even Jesus, has to be standing on the ledge of the tallest building in town, looking down and ready to leap before we stake our claim and say yes, *Yes, this is me. I am, for whatever good or bad it means, I am who I am.*

Who knows? Maybe taking that lonely journey is the only religious thing a person can do.

————

Tues, 19 Nov
Dear Mom & Dad—

In his first letter after the silence, one detail makes the otherwise business-as-usual letter chilling. . . .

Things here have been busy for the last few days—
I have a new job temporarily—The story is much too
long to try to explain but, in short, I am working in
Bde HQ as Arty Liaison because the man that was
supposed to take this job was hurt about 5 days
ago! We are waiting to see how soon he comes
back. . . .

There is no mention of the man's ever coming back.

————

Besides this—and the frequent massive omission of the fact that he is in a war at all—there are few other clues to Paul's changing perspective. *Time has been going fast* becomes . . .

It feels like I've been here a lifetime. . . .

. . . and, in a way, he had been.

By March, his life, the only life he had ever really fully imagined for himself, was over.

0004 hrs 17 March

Dear Mom & Dad,

This will be a short note since it is getting late. I
am sitting in the 1st Bde TOC and wearing a .45
pistol & flak vest (armored jacket) and helmet, the
normal duty uniform. It is extremely noisy around
here with Artillery outgoing on suspected enemy
locations and 12 radios blaring away with units in
the field. Actually, it is quite interesting but it's not
for me. I've made my decision and will stand by it.
I'm submitting my resignation from the Army
shortly....

*It's not for me...*
For the kid who had written to Senator Keating asking
for an appointment to West Point just for a chance to prove
himself, this could not have been an easy letter to write.

As for my service record, I have had excellent &
superior efficiency reports in all categories and they
tell me I qualify for:

1 Bronze Star w/"V" for valor in the face of an armed
enemy;

1 Bronze Star for achievement;

1 Army Commendation medal for outstanding service;

3 Air medals for logging flight time in a combat
zone;

1 Silver Star for valor in the face of an armed foe...

As he goes on to explain why he wants to leave the
army, he worries his explanation will not be understood...

*I just realized that you may start thinking that I'm cracking up....But no, he says. Don't worry about me. I'm not. I'm in great shape....*

What he thinks will be misinterpreted as a lack of mental stability is one of the sanest statements in all the letters: *All goes well,* my brother says, *all goes well except that...*

> I increasingly dislike trying to kill people—no matter whether they're enemies or not.

———

This, in fact, *did* make the Army think Paul was cracking up.

> April 14. Well I'm going to spend a night in Lai Khe tomorrow. I have to report to the Division Artillery Commander for counseling—he wants to try to persuade me from leaving the service....

Paul would not be persuaded. Still—

> May 13. I've been extended in the Army "for a period not to exceed 18 months." Only time will tell, and as you say, Dad, Everything happens for the best!...

———

Eventually it took Paul a lot longer than 18 months to get out of the Army.

In all that time, he never did write home about what happened in that last week of October. The closest he got was, I think, a single sentence in a letter he wrote to a very close friend who had written him condemning the war.

Paul's response, by the way, made me glad that I had not been writing him much. . . .

Johnny Neilsen, the undoubted star of the PAL baseball team, wrote Paul condemning either the war or a battle of the war. (Having only Paul's response, I can't quite tell which.) They were close enough friends that Paul was planning on sharing an apartment with him when he got out of the service, so it seems to me that Johnny would be the most likely person in the world for my brother to be open with.

But he wasn't.

Johnny's letter just left him feeling more isolated. *I guess maybe I won't fit into civilian society for a while,* he says, even as he is fitting less and less well into the military life for which he was being highly decorated.

He doesn't tell Johnny the same things that he doesn't tell Mom and Dad.

He doesn't say that, in that week without a letter, he and his men were in the bush. That before calling it a night, they would routinely fire into the dark as a final check to see if there were any stray enemy around. He doesn't say that on one night in late October—Halloween night, in fact—as they fired into the dark for the usual "mad minute," they found themselves unexpectedly smack in the middle of the "major thrust" the *New York Times* described, surrounded by a battalion of enemy—an enemy on whom it was his usual job to call in artillery strikes from a distance. He doesn't give the details of what it is that makes you increasingly dislike trying to kill people—whether they're enemies or not—as you fight for your life and the lives of your men with that same enemy at close quarters all through the night. . . .

What Paul does say is very simple, just one sentence that, in the best biblical tradition, combines ancient contradictions to speak a new truth...a truth that the Bible, that book of endless and enthusiastic war, desperately needs...

He says simply:

No one hates war more than a soldier.

———

The ceremony in which I was ordained a priest had drums and trumpets, ornate vestments, and all the trappings of medieval splendor.

It was, in every way, the exact opposite of the religious life we had developed over a decade of constant and demanding improvisation. Still, the key moment in the ceremony, the moment that makes you a priest, is very simple, very naked, and very much in harmony with the simplicity we had been reaching for through the difficult years of our training.

The act of ordination is a wordless gesture. The bishop places his hands on your head and it is done. You are a priest forever. Forget the drums and trumpets, forget the vestments, forget everything...except the touch. You are touched by hands that have been touched by hands that were touched by hands, moving back through time, touched by Christ himself. Your commission, as a priest, is to spend the rest of your life passing on that touch. It is, ultimately, a very intimate moment.

The first people you pass that touch on to is your family in your "first blessing." I know Mom and Dad felt all the love and intimacy that was in that centuries-old blessing. With my brother, who could have used a blessing, I'm not sure it took. I wanted it to. But the distance between us was too great for even Christ to bridge and, of course, there's a limit to how seriously you can take your little brother, no matter how seriously he takes himself.

———

I think of my ordination as the Last Great Party because all of our friends were there, including Johnny and the PAL team.

It was the *Last* Great Party because the following year, Dad got sick and, the year after that, he died.

(Paul had been out of the army for some years by then. He stayed longer than he had intended. The army knew a good teacher when it saw one and had kept him in for ten years. With ten years accumulated, Dad wanted Paul to stay for another ten so he could get his pension—by which point Paul would have lost his mind, teaching, as he was, the calculus of atomic destruction. So, with his wife Janet's encouragement, Paul defied Dad, left the service, went his own way, and became a teacher in a dirt poor school in El Paso, Texas. When baby Nancy came along, he supplemented the family income by night-managing a 7-Eleven, which was never robbed, Paul says, only because he knew the name of every kid in the school.)

The Last Great Family Fight *wasn't* the night before Dad died, but I remember it that way. It must have been a week or so earlier, and I don't remember who started it, but Mom and Paul went for each other. Paul came from the heart and Mom from the head. I remember Paul crying that the only person who ever loved him was in the bedroom dying. Mom, instead of saying she felt the exact same way, which would have ended the whole thing, became extremely rational and listed every god damn thing she had ever given up so Paul could have the education he never wanted.

All in all it was a pretty good fight.

Mom has the temperament, but Paul had the training so they were fairly well-matched. I was accused of being the favored son, but I decided early to sit this one out. I think, at some level, we all knew we were all just mad that Dad was dying.

I said the funeral.

We all said goodbye to Dad and then we said goodbye to one another.

Then, long after Dad had died, my brother's name finally did turn up in the *New York Times*.

———

I read the *Times* to wake up in the morning.

I probably should read the Gospels, but I don't. I read the *Times*. Blame it on my haphazard training. One morning, before going over to say the early Mass, I sat down at the breakfast table opposite another priest in the community who was reading the National section. We exchanged nods, but no words, because John—a good priest and a holy man—is, in the morning, just plain mean.

Careful not to disturb him or the silence, I took another section of the paper.

After some time, John looked up and, out of the blue, asked, *Is your brother's first name Paul?* I said yes and he, without explanation, went back to reading the paper. I was intrigued, but knew if I asked him for an explanation, he would only growl and, an accomplished passive-aggressive, read slower. So I returned to my section of the paper and waited for him to finish.

(I was back living in New York City by this time and stayed in touch with Paul—in El Paso—mostly through Mom—in Syracuse. Dad's last request to Mom was, *Take care of Paul,* and, from a distance, she tried. Letters, phone calls, occasional visits, but El Paso is a long way away and Paul remained the mystery he had been since coming home from Vietnam years before. *Mary, you've got to be patient,* Dad had said in the worst days after Paul's return, but, by this point, patience was becoming resignation to never again really knowing Paul as a son, a brother, a friend. It was a measure of Paul's mystery that, even after long three-way conversations with him, Mom would ask me. *Well, how do you think he is?)*

John looked up from the National section a few more times, each time with a more specific question. *Does your brother live in Texas?* I nodded. John went back to the paper. *Does he teach at a school named Ysleta?* A nod. Then, when he was good and finished, John slid the paper to me and said *There's an article about your brother in the* New York Times *this morning.* He left and I read...

### Top University Taps Rare Well of Talent
### At Decaying School

Special to the New York Times
El Paso, April 5
Ysleta High School is decaying and its students are mostly poor, but it has produced the largest single contingent of Hispanic Students ever to gain admission to the Massachusetts Institute of Technology from a general-attendance public high school.

I had visited Paul's school several times and liked it a lot. By this time, I was also teaching in a poor Latino school—Nativity Mission on Manhattan's Lower East Side—so teaching was something we had in common. We both enjoyed the fact that, after our very different journeys, we had ended up doing the exact same thing. I read on, delighted to see that the school was getting national press but thinking it was an exaggeration to call this an article about my brother...

M.I.T. rarely accepts more than two students from the same public high school in one year, but this year five Hispanic students from Ysleta won admission, said Joe Jasso, assistant director of admissions at the university.

Race or ethnic background are not considerations in the selection process, he said. The university in Cambridge, Mass., admits only about 1,000 of the 7,000 students who apply each year, he said. About 600 enroll.

Roger Parks, the principal of Ysleta High, said, "We're on the wrong side of the freeway, and we have as high a dropout rate as any school in the area. But we don't fit the stereotype," he said. "The school is more than this ratty old building. The school is a personality, a soul."

Mr. Parks noted that other Ysleta graduates have attended M.I.T. as well as Harvard, Yale, Vassar and the University of Southern California. Ninety-five percent of the school's 6,000 students are of Hispanic background.

Tony Marquez, an El Paso education consultant for M.I.T. who approved the five admissions, said that the families of three students had incomes below the poverty level and that it would be difficult for any to attend an out-of-town college without financial aid.

Three things the five students have in common, Mr. Parks said, are strong scientific and mathematical skill and one teacher: Paul Cain, an instructor in computer mathematics...

This was one of the few times in my life when I found myself crying before I knew it was happening.

I went back, read the passage again and continued...

Three things the five students have in common, Mr. Parks said, are strong scientific and mathematical skill and one teacher: Paul Cain, an instructor in computer mathematics.

"They gravitate to him, and with him they build themselves to a competitive edge," Mr. Parks said.

But Mr. Cain said that the parents of the five students deserve most of the credit for their children's accomplishment....

The article went on very nicely about the kids, but Roger Parks, principal and fellow Vietnam veteran, had seen to it that, somehow, it *was* an article about my brother, an announcement in no uncertain terms about what he had become, where his journey had finally taken him.

I finished the article, got up and went over to the Church of St. Francis Xavier, my parish church, the church attached to the Jesuit military school that I had followed my brother into years before, where both of us feel our courses in life were set.

I said Mass and I preached to the morning congregation everything I know about religion. I told them the story of my brother's life.

———

### JANUARY 31

I save too many letters.

Over the year, I toss them in a box and, around New Year's, I reread and file them.

I should throw them out, but, every now and then, when friends are in trouble, I like sending them back some of their old letters. They are invariably amazed at how good they were in hard times past...or how funny...or smart ...or how unexpectedly brave....

And they always—always—have the same question. They ask, *If the letters meant so much to you, why the hell didn't you answer them?*

———

I have read Paul's letters many times and I *still* haven't answered them.

I could write him now.

I have a perfect excuse. He was on CNN again tonight discussing education.

Mom, who is supposed to be dying, couldn't have been more alive watching him tonight. She is, as she always has been, a little in awe of him, especially now that he has turned out to be so much more than she could have envisioned. And, even though she beamed watching Paul on TV, I know she has still never found a way to convey to him her total approval...and that is probably a very good thing. Who knows what new hidden burdens might lurk encoded in an expression of unconditional love? That will just have to be part of her unfinished journey.

I don't know what I could say to my brother that would express my admiration and love.

Thank you for not murdering me in my crib?

Thank you for letting me ride on the back of your bike?

Thank you for always counting me among your friends?

Thank you for all those letters I never answered?

If I were to write to Paul, I know I would send him the sign Dad lettered to welcome him home.

And the map that was on the wall.

Both have been carefully saved along with the letters.

I think he might understand from them that Dad was carrying him in his heart every inch of the way....

And, I suppose, I could send these pages along with them.

When my friends ask why I didn't answer their letters, I always say the same thing. I say, *What could I possibly have written that would, even remotely, match the beauty of what you had already written?*

I could offer my brother his own words back to him— hoping he'd see in them his greatness, his beauty, the holiness of his journey....

Alaska, 6 May, Sunday
Dear Mom & Dad,
Spring has sprung...

Letters. Just letters.

I sat out in the sun today for about four hours
working and it was great. I don't think anybody has
appreciated the sun until they have spent a winter
in Alaska!

Like Philippians, Galatians, Corinthians, taking the story a little deeper into the heart of the mystery, where heat, denied any outlet, turns coal into diamonds....

I still haven't received any orders so I'll be waiting
again this week....

### Chapter 12. The Lost Epistle of Paul

Letter writing is a dying art and perhaps that's a shame.

*The Email of St. Paul to the Romans* doesn't have the same ring to it as *The Epistle.*

And *St. Paul's First Tweet to the Corinthians* doesn't work at all.

But there is still power in our communications.

I received an email from a friend of almost fifty years that hit me with the force of revelation. I will quote it in its entirety after a later chapter.

I mention it here to say that I firmly believe that there is revelation flashing back and forth among us all the time.

If we look...

# 13

# How God Prays

## Prayer—Part 2
### MAY 20

*Billy, does God answer prayers?*

Well, either he does or he doesn't, but I never expected to hear my mother ask me the question.

As a priest, I would usually take a question about prayer seriously, but, since I've never been much of a priest to my family, I joked when Mom asked *Does God answer prayers?* I said *Well, that's what you always told me.*

But she wasn't joking.

She continued *Because I'm praying all the time...and he doesn't answer my prayers.* Taking her more seriously now, I asked what she was praying for. She said simply *To get better.* After a pause, I suggested that maybe she should pray for something else. She asked *Like what?...*

*Well,* I said, *to enjoy every day that comes as much as you possibly can* and she shook her head and said, *No, you don't understand....*

I understand better than she thinks. I, too, have cancer.

I have cancer.

————

Well, either I have cancer or I don't.

My cancer hasn't been diagnosed yet. In fact, I haven't even seen the doctor yet. But I know I have it. I even know what kind I have. Viral. I have viral cancer. I know cancer isn't viral. I know that. I know that *most* cancer isn't viral; mine is. I caught it from Mom. I should have been more careful. Worn a mask. Sterilized the silverware. Something to protect myself. And I know—I know I know I KNOW—this is insane but knowing I am suffering from hypochondria does NOT mean that I DON'T have cancer! Nor does it stop me from waking up in the night so acutely aware that cancer is growing inside me that I can barely breathe. And since there is no way I can go back to sleep (I don't even want to, the nightmares are so awful), I lie on my bed and pray that most desperate of serenity prayers, *Lord Jesus Christ have mercy on me a sinner.*

*Lord Jesus Christ, have mercy on me a sinner. . . . Lord Jesus Christ, have mercy on me a sinner. . . . Lord Jesus Christ . . .* I pray the prayer over and over until it becomes a single word endlessly repeated. *Lordjesuschristhavemercyonmeasinner . . .* and I pray and I pray and I'm praying like a bastard but it's not helping.

————

Well, I am either praying or I am not praying.

I have the strong suspicion that my mother and I aren't praying at all. I think what we are calling prayer is just plea bargaining in the face of a death sentence, hers more immediate than mine, but mine eventually just as real. Either way, I will tell you this: even if the cancer isn't real, the nightmares and night terrors are, and acute anxiety and a growing sleep deficit are making me very hard to live with.

Mom, I should also point out, is not helping much by smoking in the house.

I tell her that—beside the fact that the doctor doesn't want her to smoke—her second-hand smoke is a danger to me since, based on her and Dad's health histories, I have a genetic predisposition to cancer. On top of that, her smoking triggers my hypochondria and drives me into panic attacks.

Mom listens carefully and then asks, *What does this have to do with me, Billy? I gave up smoking years ago.*

————

Mom either gave up smoking years ago or she didn't.

When I ask her about the smell of cigarette smoke in the house, she says *Cathy smokes when she comes to clean. What can I say, Billy? She's so good to me. I can't tell her no.* All winter long I have suggested she might ask Cathy to step outside when she smokes and Mom has said, rightly. *Are you crazy? It's minus thirty degrees wind chill, Billy!*

Now my mother is either lying about smoking or she isn't.

So, since my mother, in general, doesn't lie (which makes her completely useless at screening calls), I choose to believe her and search for the cigarettes only when she is sleeping.

————

Mom's doctor, Dr. P, says Mom could live for years—even five years.

Mom doesn't buy it. *Billy, I just don't feel that good.* Mom's friend Paulette, meanwhile, is furious that the doctor still asks Mom come to his office to see him. *Doesn't he see that she can't do this? That it's too hard? And why isn't he taking care of the pain? It's criminal!* Paulette pushes me to get hospice set up for Mom because the hospice people are very good with pain management. But to get into hospice you have to be reasonably sure that you will die within six months and Mom won't have the necessary CAT scan that would tell how the cancer is progressing. (Me, I'd *love* a CAT scan to find out how my imaginary cancer is doing, but does anyone offer? No.) Mom would rather just cope with the pain day by day and that's exactly what we do because the doctor—assuming that Mom will live for years—is very conservative with pain medication. So we were startled during a doctor's visit (March 25th) when, after Mom makes a case for more medication—with her carefully annotated 3x5 cards charting her pills against her pain—Dr. P said *Let's not play around with this anymore. Let's start your mother on morphine.* I suppose this is what we have been asking for, but it sends a chill through us because of what happened with Dad and morphine.

———

I eventually go to New York to see my doctor.

When I explain about the viral cancer, he laughs, not unkindly, and says, *Well, now that we have the diagnosis, maybe you could describe your symptoms.* I tell him my aches and pains. I tell him about the night terrors and, as he examines me, he asks me if I have ever been through anything like this before? And I say, *I have . . . Dad had just been put on morphine. . . .*

———

Dad had coped with pain for a long time on Demerol and distractions.

The Demerol was good, but distractions—especially visits from family and friends—were best.

Dad's brother Bill, the most gently charming of Dad's five brothers, would come every afternoon and sit with Dad for hours, freeing Mom up to do her chores. And his brother Bobby (Wobbles) would stop by. And there were wonderful surprise visits—like the time the buzzer rang. *Mary, it's Tom. Let me in, and OH MY GOD! PETE, PETE! IT'S TOM!* and in came Dad's roommate from college who, the second he heard Pete was sick, jumped in his car and drove four hundred miles, arriving unannounced but sure of his welcome, to continue the running party that had been their friendship for fifty years—a party raucous enough, by the way, to get them both thrown out of college.

(After they finally graduated, they were both grateful they had been thrown out for a time since, while they were away, the main classroom building burned down and, if they had been there, they were sure it would have been blamed on them.)

(No college for Mom, by the way. She went to Vocational High and *I got work the day I graduated, Billy. No, not the day after, the day I graduated. I went to work that day, graduated that night.* She didn't resent not having gone to college, but she did, from time to time, use the fact that we had gone against us. When something would be hopelessly out of whack in the house—usually one of the prac-

tical things she was so good at—she'd say, *Now what COL-
LEGE GRADUATE did this!)*

Visits, such as Mom's friend Paulette arriving with
home-made applesauce, were lifesavers.

But by the time that Pete, the good dresser, could no longer
fit in his clothes and had shrunk so much that we had to
buy him a very soft chair and line that with an even softer
sheepskin to keep him from bruising on his own bones, by
then, even visits weren't much help.

Though the day Mike Sala, a friend of mine, hiker of the
Appalachian Trail and the picture of health, arrived and
asked—without greeting us—*Where's Mr. Cain?*, walked
into the bedroom and threw his arms around my shrunken
father was a pretty damn good day, pain or no pain.

Yet after a while, distractions ceased to help.

Dad's description of his pain was chilling and it stays
with me. *It's like they're boring a hole through me,* he said. Dad
was always a person to make the best of everything. If he
heard an ambulance he would always say *There's a baby on
the way!* He would stare at a patch of lawn until he found a
four-leaf clover. *All things work together unto the good* was his
motto, but there was no good in this. *It's like they're boring a
hole through me, Billy.*

So the doctor put him on morphine. . . .

Dad, who liked the good things in life, liked morphine.

Even though he hated the injections the nurse gave him
every four hours (there was very little flesh on his bones
and the needle hurt him every time), still the morphine was
miraculous and Dad looked forward to it.

We did not.

After the shot, there would be a short period of
supreme contentment during which Dad was his old pre-
pain, pre-cancer self. After that, he...he wouldn't exactly

sleep. His eyes would be open but he wouldn't be seeing us. He would drift away with a quiet smile on his face. He would sit in his big soft chair and move his hands like he was conducting a silent orchestra. He'd reach out like someone weightless in space, amused by something floating just slightly beyond his grasp. And he might as well have been in outer space, he was so far away from us. He had left us behind for some private happiness we could not be part of. And we, who loved him and relied on him and been fine as long as we could talk to him, suddenly felt very, very abandoned. We, who cried very little, began to cry a lot.

Then we did a very deeply stupid—maybe even an evil—thing.

We were a family that had always been honest with one another, and I suppose we didn't realize that even honesty has its limits. One summer Friday afternoon, if not evilly, at least foolishly, Mom and I told Dad how much we missed him since he had started on the morphine shots. We didn't ask him anything, but he understood what we wanted and he said, without pause, *Okay, let's go back to the Demerol then.*

And we did.

With Dad's consent, we canceled the nurse for the weekend and went back to the Demerol.

We knew in less than four hours that this was a terrible mistake.

Dad's pain before had been unbearable, but this was worse, because not only was it unbearable, it was unnecessary. We had asked Dad to have this pain so we could be together. You know what we learned? We learned we weren't worth it. And, as painful as that was, it was nowhere near as painful as knowing that we were putting this man whom we loved through terrible pain. But, as we had not asked anything of Dad, he asked nothing of us. He looked at us through his pain and we looked at him. There was nothing to say. Then Mom stood up, went to the phone, called the doctor and asked to reverse her request. She was told that no nurse was available for the weekend, but Dad could resume the morphine on Monday. This sent terror through us all. I remember Mom not getting an answer when she asked Dad, *Can you make it till Monday, Pete?* Mom called the doctor back immediately and asked if she could give the shots herself and the doctor said certainly, if there was someone who could show her how. Mom hung up the phone and called Dorothy B.

Dorothy, the apartment-complex-snoop and busybody, was also a retired nurse and magnificent when given the chance to focus her endless energy on a worthy task.

She showed Mom how to give the shots. Later when the doctor asked Mom if she had practiced on an orange, she replied, *No, Doctor, I practiced on the patient,* and they all, including Dad, laughed.

And so, we watched him drift away again and again. We resented his going and Dad resented his returning and the meeting time in between got shorter and shorter. Worse, in that precious in-between time, Dad began to blame Mom for the pain of the needles. *Pete, I wouldn't cause you pain for the world,* Mom would say, and then go cry in the kitchen. Eventually I explained the situation to Dad, so, when Mom came in and gave him what was clearly a terribly painful shot, and Dad said with a smile, *Mary, that was the best one yet,* Mom left the room on cloud nine. Dad then turned to me and winked. He winked, as if to say, *We're going to be all right. All things work together unto the good.*

Then he drifted away again.

It was a hard time.

———

Dad's actual death wasn't all that hard.

I had left for a weekend to do a wedding of two of my friends—I can be a priest to non-family members—and Paul had just left for El Paso after a visit. When I got home, I was met at the airport by two of my father's brothers— Bobby and the ever-faithful Bill. Bobby told me quietly that Dad had died just before they came to get me. When we got to baggage claim, Uncle Bill took me aside and, a bit deaf, he told me, *Billy I know Wobbles isn't telling you this. But I think you should know—your dad died,* and he gave me the details all over again. This would have made Dad laugh.

The apartment, when I got there, was chaos. There were more people there than there had been in weeks. I couldn't even get to Mom who was sitting looking baffled in the kitchen. I threw everybody out. *Now! Out! Everybody, out!* (If anybody minded, I never heard about it.) And I sat down with Mom to hear her version of what had happened.

*It was peaceful, Billy. We were around him. Me and Dorothy and we were praying and he was quiet. And he just stopped breathing. So peaceful. Dorothy checked his pulse and his heart and he was gone. Pete was gone.*

There was no sorrow in this telling. There was gratitude that it had been so easy finally. And there was pride. *He wanted to die at home, Billy, and he did.* He did. *I did everything I could.* And she did.

I didn't tell the doctor who was examining me all of this. I did tell him this:

The weeks before he died, I didn't think I could get much closer to my father.

I was pretty much carrying him wherever he needed to go, attending to all his needs. And this was fine, in fact, a privilege.... Then one night I found myself sleeping with him.

That afternoon, while Mom and I were in the living room, Dad fell out of bed and gave himself a gash across the forehead. The fall wasn't serious, but it scared all of us—Dad included—very badly. Until we could get a hospital bed with sides that we could raise, we would protect Dad through the night by having one side of his bed against the wall; Dad would sleep next to the wall and I would sleep on the outside of the bed. (To get any sleep at all, Mom was, by now, sleeping on the couch.)

During the nights of sleeping with Dad, I had the most horrible nightmares of my life. Cancer appeared in the dream as a living, conscious, inescapably malevolent being —a huge, burning cigarette ash hanging in the middle of a room, glowing from within like an illuminated skull. It was slowly and knowingly sucking all the oxygen out of the room to keep its own dark fire burning while the rest of us were choking helplessly before it.

And this was all there was.

The world was cancer—nothing but cancer.

I woke up with an unshakable conviction that I was dying of cancer.

This, finally, is what I tell the doctor.

My doctor, after completing the exam, tells me that hypochondria is perfectly normal when dealing with death. It happens to medical students all the time. When he sees I don't believe him, the doctor, a good and kind man, puts his forehead practically against mine and says slowly, *You–Do–Not–Have–Cancer.*

That night, when my friends ask how the doctor's visit went, I say, *Bad news. The doctor couldn't find the cancer.*

The visit to the doctor, my one hope of sanity, had failed.

———

Mom and I sit at the kitchen table looking at our little bottle of liquid morphine.

Though Mom and I have never discussed Dad's progression on morphine, I know she has thought about it.

Last December when the doctor increased her pain medication from a pill every four hours to one every three, Mom was initially delighted. *Billy, I slept all the way to five in the morning. Isn't that great?* Yes, but she also slept through much of the next day, didn't get her puzzles done, and missed all her shows, and this troubled her. I am sure she was thinking of Dad when she decided to go back to the old dosage . . . and discovered that she couldn't.

With the care of alchemists, we measure ten morphine drops from an eye-dropper—no needles this time, thank God—into a teaspoon. The morphine is then added to applesauce.

(Every medicine has its own medium: ice cream for Darvocet, prune juice for the sleeping medication, etc. Only the heart medication is taken in straightforward pill form, so it's the only one I don't supervise. This, in retrospect, was a mistake. Or not.)

Mom raises the spoon in a toast *Well, here goes nothing,* takes it, and, to our astonishment, it works. Perfectly. The doctor tells us we are very lucky. This exact form of the medication at a very low dosage seems to address Mom's pain receptors perfectly and leave her alert.

There are still problems, of course. Mom still has horrible choking spells, and, more seriously, the dosage wears off quickly, but the doctor says we can mix and match the morphine at strictly regulated intervals with the earlier pain medication as needed. Occasionally, there are major pain episodes, but, in general, Mom is feeling much better. Instead of disappearing as Dad had, Mom is more there and more able to go about her life. There is more conversation in the house—even joking. (Mom accuses me of over-dosing her to get to watch my TV shows when they conflict with hers.) She's been able to get out to get her hair done, and whatever the hell happens at the beauty parlor is defi-nitely prayer. Things are going fine. Who knows? Maybe Mom *will* live another five years. Why not? She is feeling much better.

In fact, she feels well enough to smoke.

———

After my session with the doctor failed to bring me any peace, I was even more brittle than before.

One day I came back from the store early, went to Mom's bathroom to replace the toilet paper and found it full of smoke.

Determined to be reasonable, I go into the kitchen and say, *Look, Mom everything is going well. Let's stick with the pro-gram, OK?*

Mom, knowing exactly what I am talking about, says, *What in the world are you talking about, Billy?*

I say, *The bathroom's FULL of smoke and Cathy hasn't been here for a WEEK. What's the story? Are you trying to turn me into a junior high school bathroom monitor?*

I can see Mom trying to figure out her best tactic.

She chooses to go on the offensive.

She says, *Now, Billy, I've been watching TV very carefully and there is no conclusive proof that second-hand smoke is harmful to anybody.*

This pushes me right over the brink. *Are you really siding with the BIG TOBACCO COMPANIES against YOUR OWN SON?!* And she says, *NOW DON'T SHOUT AT ME! I'M NOT DOING ANYTHING AGAINST YOU! I'M JUST DOING WHAT YOU TOLD ME TO DO!* And I say, *WHAT I TOLD*

*YOU TO DO? WHAT I TOLD YOU TO DO? WHAT ARE YOU TALKING ABOUT? I SPECIFICALLY ASKED YOU NOT TO...* and she interrupts, *BILLY, YOU TOLD ME I SHOULD ENJOY EVERY DAY AS MUCH AS I COULD. DIDN'T YOU? WELL, DIDN'T YOU?*

And I did.

And, seeing I am speechless, she sits back with a triumphant smile and says again, *Well, didn't you?*

She clearly had been saving that one up for some time.

What can I say?

She is perfectly right.

So I simply announce that I am going on strike until the cigarettes are out of the house and I go to my room and I shut the door.

————

We had a bad night.

Even though the house rule is that nobody goes to bed angry, we weren't speaking much while I got her medications ready that night.

*Maybe tomorrow will be a better day,* Mom said as she went to bed.

————

As soon as she is in bed, I scour the apartment.

I look everywhere for the cigarettes.

Everywhere.

I tear the place apart.

When I finally find them (with her old medications — which makes a Mary-Cain sort of sense, I should have thought of that) I have a feeling of triumph.

The light is still on in Mom's bedroom, the news radio station is still rehashing the events of the day, and I am glad Mom is still up.

I go into her room, cigarettes in hand, to announce that I have found them and that I have her dead to rights!

And once I am in the room, I stop.

————

Her head is on the pillow and her eyes are open, but she isn't awake.

Her wide-open eyes are looking at me, but she isn't seeing me.

In fact, her eyes are rolling slightly.

Her hands are moving gracefully through the air.

For the first time, the morphine—I suppose it's the cumulative effect—has Mom drifting away.

————

Strange.

I sit on the end of her bed for a while.

Strange how alone I feel.

I would not feel this alone if she were sleeping.

I go into the living room and sit for a long time.

I sit quietly because I can feel a prayer forming in me and I don't want to disturb it.

A real prayer—no maybe-it-is and maybe-it-isn't about it.

————

I can feel the prayer forming itself in me.

Something kind.

Something that doesn't care if it lives or dies.

Something free—like Tom's four-hundred-mile drive and Mike's embrace and Dad's in-spite-of-the-pain wink. And as it forms in me, it makes me laugh and is completely wrong and still it's prayer anyway. Real prayer. Not the words we say or the bargains we make with God, but Paulette's applesauce and Uncle Bill's constant presence. Prayers that don't even think about being answered because they aren't questions. Prayers that, deeply generous, are their own answers. And I think maybe this is the kind of prayer that God prays.

———

I stand up from the couch.

I take the cigarettes and, knowing that she will continue to smoke and it will be bad for her and knowing that I will continue to pretend not to know where the cigarettes are and that we will continue to fight about them and Mom, knowing she has a winning line, will continue to insist, *You told me to enjoy every day as much as I could! Didn't you? Well, didn't you?*—knowing all this, I put the cigarettes back in their hiding place.

———

And that is my prayer for the day.

Then I go bed and sleep well for the first time in weeks.

## Chapter 13. How God Prays

My father prayed on his knees every night before bed. I was always impressed by that. But I was equally impressed, even startled, when one freezing cold night when I was very young, Dad was driving the family down a Manhattan street near the Bowery—fashionable now— then skid row. He stopped the car and said, "I'll be right back."

He walked back a few car lengths and helped a man who had been sleeping on the street to a hallway. He opened the door and brought the man in. After making sure the man was warm, he came back to the car and we drove on. Not a word said.

In the face of death, my mother's friends made applesauce, gave car rides, wrote cards, shopped for food and specialty items, clipped articles, called to talk, visited, called to say there was a show on she might like, brought lilacs. . . . My mother loved lilacs.

I don't think what emerges from the depths of God in God's prayer is words. I suspect it is more like lilacs.

What else, I wonder, emerges silently from the depths of prayer?

## 14

# What's the Point of the Bible?

Six months ago, the doctor said my mother had six months to live.

Now, as the sixth month passes, questions arise. Some are the usual self-interested chatter that jabbers on in the back of my mind. *How long will this go on? What about me? What about my life?* But bigger questions arise as well. The biggest being *Why? Why must she be in this pain? Why must there be so much suffering? Why do we grow old? Why?*

Are there answers to such questions?

As one long day made clear, there is an answer to one question.

I am writing this to save the stories.

Now I know why this matters.

————

The specific story I'm saving here is one of Mom's, which is odd because Dad was the master storyteller of the family. His stories were sinuous, twisty, and never told the same way twice. A typical story from Dad would wander all over town.

194

Mom's stories, on the other hand, were rigidly structured. They all went pretty much the same way:

a. Times were tough.
b. We worked hard.
c. Things got better.

Mom's a.b.c. story structure isn't a bad one. It is the basis for Mom's favorite book and movie, *Gone with the Wind*. My mother loves Scarlett O'Hara. Loves her for her beauty, for her romances, but mostly because *My, she was such a hard worker, Billy!* The plot of *Gone with the Wind*, if my mother had to summarize it, would go like this:

a. The Civil War—Oh! Times were hard.
b. Scarlett O'Hara—she worked very hard;
c. Things got better.

———

Mom's condition had recently stabilized—a new pain medication was, for the moment, working—so I went on a long-postponed business trip to California. Dutifully, I called Mom every day and, dutifully, every day she told me how well she was doing. So well, in fact, that, with her blessing, I extended the trip a week for some much-needed vacation.

When I walked back in the door after two weeks away, my mother looked so old, so utterly defeated, that I knew three things instantly: I knew she had been lying to me on the phone about how well she was doing. I knew I had known she was lying. And I knew how grateful I was to her for her lies.

And I thought, *Well, this is finally it. This is the beginning of my mother's dying.*

Something terrible had happened in my absence, but, most uncharacteristically, she wouldn't tell me what. All she would offer was, *Things are bad. What can I say?*

From her bed that night she said, not especially to me, *I've held myself together as long as I can. I guess I just can't do it anymore.*

————

It was the "As God is my witness, I'll never be hungry again" scene that iced Mom's connection with Scarlett. Mom, like Scarlett, was wounded by the shame of poverty and had made similar vows. Her association with a survivor's story served her well.

The story worked for her. Protected her. Comforted her. Told her what to do. Most of us, I think, do the same. We make of our fundamental wounds some version of our life story that converts our weaknesses into strengths and sustains us.

(David Copperfield, by the way, was a liar. He knew who was going to be the hero of his own life story. We all do.)

The loss of her father—a beautiful man in the few pictures we have of him whom she resembles closely—and a childhood of poverty were Mom's wounds. Hard work was for her the solution that would save her. She would never be hungry again.

I got my first hint about what had happened in my absence the next day when Mom's cleaning lady-and-psychotherapist Cathy whispered to me, as soon as Mom left the room, *Your mother should be in a nursing home and you know it.* There was an edge of panic in her voice I did not understand. When I said *But she wouldn't be happy in a…*

Cathy answered, *It doesn't MATTER about her happiness anymore!* Then—at considerable cost to herself—she said, *Billy, she–can't–keep–herself–CLEAN–anymore!*

———

Neil, Mom's brother, who grew up in the same poverty, had no such story to protect him.

His was supposed to be the story of the gifted athlete who goes to college and returns a sports hero. It never happened. He went to college, alright, but he had to return almost immediately to help support the family. After that he was a man without a story.

Of course, I only know this from my mother's version of the family story. It might look very different from Neil's side. But I do know that my mother's version gave her an energy that lasted a lifetime.

It is important to have a story.

———

*Billy, she–can't–keep–herself–CLEAN–anymore.*

Cathy then goes on to describe "soiled" undergarments that she has found hidden deep in the hamper. Now Cathy, a plain-spoken person, has no trouble using the word *shit*, but the word that she uses now is "soiled," though "soil" is not what we are talking about. *Billy, it's time for a nursing home.*

I find I don't have a lot of patience for Cathy's panicked overreaction. Still, I think, if anybody has a right to overreact, it's Cathy. She has taken extraordinary responsibility for my mother, especially while I was away. I try to reassure her by telling her that we will get more help. Cathy wants to know, *How?*

I would offer to help myself but it won't work. In our mostly male household, the bathroom was always Mom's sanctuary. My brother, my father, and I could all use our tiny bathroom at the same time like a well-rehearsed Marx Brothers' routine, but it was Mom's one place of privacy. So all the bathroom things that I found easy to do for Dad are simply impossible with Mom.

I tell Cathy I will talk to Dr. P about getting home health aides and she is satisfied, though I know Mom will not like that. At all.

Home health aides, or aides of any kind, do not figure into my mother's story.

Mom, whose heart was weakened by childhood rheumatic fever, always assumed she would die like her mother, Johanna Dawson, who scrubbed floors and took in wash her whole life. Not feeling well one day, Johanna went to bed, fell asleep, and never got up again. In Mom's terms, this was "a beautiful death." That's how the story is supposed to go. You work till you can't and then you die without causing anybody any trouble. But, as with Neil, the story doesn't always go the way it is supposed to.

———

Dr. P listens carefully as I describe the situation as delicately as I can, emphasizing our need for help with "hygiene." The doctor nods his understanding and I go on. It is odd for me to talk this much to Dr. P, since Mom is usually in charge of these sessions. But she doesn't want to talk about this. She doesn't even want me to talk about it, but what can I do? As I speak, Dr. P repeatedly turns to Mom—sensitively, considerately—asking for her confirmation. Mom says, *Well, a little.* Or, *Not as much as he says . . .* , thus undercutting my request for help.

The doctor asks me to leave so he can examine Mom and when I am called back in, he is chipper, assuring us that this is not (as I had feared) the beginning of the end. There is a "blockage" that will have to be cleared, and this may be "uncomfortable" but it is not unexpected. The new pain medication, for which we have been so grateful, has side effects and this is one of them. As for "hygiene," although he will have to fudge the diagnosis a bit, he will request a visiting nurse weekly—starting date to be determined—and a home health aide three times a week.

This is the very best we could have hoped for. I am delighted. I look to Mom to get her reaction.

She is staring at the floor like a shamed child.

———

There was no Tara in my mother's story, just the house on Bryant Avenue where she and Neil grew up. That house was the only thing the family ever owned. Johanna managed to keep it after her husband's death by having her brother Dan (never married) and sister Lala (like Johanna, early widowed) move in and help with expenses. Through hard times, they held on to that house. It was full of memories and surrounded by lilacs....

Even now she loves lilacs more than any other flower, and there is a special place in her heart for Martha, one of Dad's nieces, who every spring brings her lilacs from her own garden.

It was here that Mom remembered herself, as a small girl, riding the family's St. Bernard through those lilacs....

And it was here that Mom, shortly after Johanna had died her beautiful death, had her fundamental wound reopened. The house, so long protected from all comers, was taken from her.

Neil, her brother, took it.

Shocked, Mom went to the parish priest, asked for advice, and was told that, since Neil already had a family and she and Pete as of yet did not, she should give him the house.

So Mary sold Neil her half of the house for a dollar.

And—as she would say on the rare occasion when she would tell the story—*And I never even got the dollar.* She stopped talking to her brother (cards at Christmas, of course, and birthdays) and she and Pete headed off to New York City where:

a. Times were tough.
b. They worked hard.
c. Things got better...

———

The morning after the visit with the doctor, in spite of all aches and pains, Mom pulls herself together and says, *I don't know how many more times I can do this, Billy,* and goes to see Gloria, her hairdresser. God knows what Gloria does, but somehow getting the hair done magically offers protection from the ravages of everything else. Mom returns, bright-eyed, completely satisfied with her (to me) absurdly sculpted hair, full of news and chat, and she walks, smiling, into an ambush.

A nurse is waiting.

The doctor has been most efficient and the "procedures" that may be "uncomfortable" will start today.

There is nothing to do but go forward, so Mom, magic draining from her eyes, takes this lovely young nurse (with latex gloves, bottles and tubes) into the sanctuary of her bathroom from which, for the next forty minutes, emerge sounds of plumbing and cries of serious pain.

All, as it turns out, for nothing.

The procedure has been unsuccessful and will have to be tried again tomorrow.

The nurse and my mother part like old friends, each feeling that she has somehow failed the other. My mother holds the nurse's hand at the door. The nurse kisses my mother on the cheek before leaving, *She's a hard worker, Billy,* for another call.

*I think I'm going to lie down on the couch for a while, Billy.* No, she doesn't want the TV on. Or the radio. When her friends call, she pretends to be asleep. When her breathing tells me that she is no longer pretending, I run the day's necessary errands hoping everything will be back to normal by the time I get back.

When I get back, there is music in the house—Mom's news-and-soft-rock station. And when she calls out, *Well, welcome back, stranger,* there is energy in her voice. Thinking that maybe things aren't as bad as they seem, I walk into the living room expecting to find her on the couch....

I don't know how long I stand, looking at the couch, before Mom calls from the kitchen in a perfectly normal voice, *I'm out here, Billy, doing the puzzle....*

I do not answer.

I do not even move.

The normalcy in Mom's voice freezes me. I suddenly find it chilling, incongruous, even offensive.... I don't know what to think, but I know what I'm feeling—a sudden visceral rush of panic and as my mind clears I hear a voice within, me say, *Oh, so THIS is what Cathy meant.* What I thought was her overreaction now seems perfectly reasonable, even understated, to me.

And it has nothing to do with the physical reality of cleaning up. I misjudged Cathy on that badly. It has much more to do with what Mom said with astonishing accuracy the night I got home from my trip. *I held myself together as long as I could, but I guess I just can't do it anymore.*

The enormous yellow/gold couch, the centerpiece of our most public space, our living room, is "soiled." Badly "soiled." As I stand there, a terrible shame arises. I do not want to see this terrible loss of control, this forfeiting of hard-won adult status, since the control that is being lost is the earliest control we exercise over the world. There is a terror in watching a person fall apart.

There is terror involved. And a deep desire to look away.

*Billy, is that you?* ... The apprehension in Mom's voice. *Billy?* finally wakes me up. *I'm here, Mom.*

I turn and walk toward kitchen, but I am stopped again. The green rug is "soiled."

In several places, "soiled." Avoiding the kitchen, I check out the apartment quickly. ... I can follow Mom's path since I left by the stains (in some cases, more than stains) on the floor ... the rugs ... the bed. I find myself disgusted by the condition of the apartment and decide to clean it up without telling Mom because if I, who care nothing for cleanliness, am this disturbed, I can only imagine what she would feel if she found out what she has done. ...

When I finally walk into the kitchen, Mom—with her absurdly sculpted hair—sits there, smiling, pleased that she has survived yet another ordeal, not knowing yet that she has, in fact, not survived. She does not see, as I do now, how badly the back of her house dress is soiled.

*Well, at least I got my hair done today.* She smiles. *That's something.*

I don't know exactly what to do or to say.

I tell her I think she ought to try going to the bathroom. She doesn't think she has to and returns to her puzzle. I say I think she ought to try.

Hearing the concern in my voice, Mom nods and, without further question, proceeds to the bathroom, where, after a long moment, *Oh, my God ... Oh, my God ...* she discovers that she had unknowingly soiled herself and then the panic hits her as well. *Oh, my God, Billy. Oh, my God ...*

I reassure her falsely and, asking if she can be left alone for a few minutes, I run to the store and grab anything that looks like it might be useful for cleaning and deodorizing. I have no idea how much stuff I have tossed into my shopping basket until the cashier asks me for more money than I have in my wallet.

When I get back, the door of Mom's bathroom is somewhat open.

*I am writing this to save a story. Not this one. But the other one will not make any sense without this one. So—*

Mom's housedress and underwear lie at her feet, too terribly soiled to be conveniently hidden in the hamper. She is straining to clean herself, one hand holding her awkwardly off the toilet, the other holding—ladylike—the small, carefully folded piece of toilet paper with which she is trying to clean herself. She is having a terrible time. Still, she never alters the dainty way in which she holds the paper in spite of the fact that she is just dirtying herself further.

I watch without thinking, judging, or processing the information.

When Mom looks up and sees me looking at her, she suddenly sees her own nakedness and her dirtiness and desperately shouts *Close the door. Close the door! CLOSE–THE–DOOR!*

The Scarlett O'Hara story got Mary Dawson Cain a long way, but Scarlett's story will never take her here and, deprived of her story, who would she be? And my mother, sitting here, stripped, dirty, shouting, who is she? Without the protection of her story, who is she, but just another helpless, shamefully exposed old lady?

And who am I, but a foolish son, all escape cut off, trapped, wishing desperately for some honorable way out of this humiliation?

*Close the door! Billy! CLOSE–THE–DOOR!*

And I would like to. I really would, but she is never going to able to clean up the mess she is in. *I SAID close the DOOR, Billy!*

*Billy, I am your MOTHER and I am TELLING YOU to CLOSE–THIS–DOOR!*

Silence.

I cross the threshold, go in and sit on the hamper facing her.

She puts her head in her hands.

Silence.

I say, *We've been through a lot.*

And she nods yes seriously.

*But—*

A moment.

*I'm afraid that this is it for modesty. We've done alright that way so far, but to get through this we are really going to have to work together, OK?*

There is very rarely silence between us, but there is silence now.

And discouragement.

And grit and will power.

And smell.

And no alternative.

*Whatever you say.*

And now we are down to the basics. Flesh and bone. And the flesh, wrinkled, scarred, hanging loosely over slack muscles, is hard to clean. Trying to work quickly only slows us down and, *Oh my God, Billy, I have to sit down.* She has to rest repeatedly, so the whole process becomes impossibly prolonged.

When she is finally clean and the house dress disposed of, Mom thinks the ordeal is over.

I know better.

I bring one of my purchases into the bathroom—an outsized box wrapped in cellophane, which I break, to remove an ugly, bulky, bilious green adult diaper. (Later one of the nurses will tell me, *Never call them diapers. Call them disposable undergarments.* And she's right, but I didn't know that then....) Mom, the good dresser, takes one look at it and says *Oh I could never use one of those, Billy, take it away.*

I insist.

She says no.

She chooses to make a last stand for her dignity here. She will not wear diapers. She just couldn't.

I know she has to.

She won't. *Bring me some underwear, Billy. Now do as I tell you. DO AS I TELL YOU!*

I think for a minute ... and then I tell her what the apartment looks like.

I tell her the condition of the living room, the rug, the bedroom, the bed, all of it. And I can hear that my voice is not level. There is blame in it. This is insane, but I can hear it.

When I finish speaking, she has not moved a muscle.

She is not looking at me, yet I know, without her making a single motion, that the final fiber of strength has gone out of her.

This strength that I have relied on so long and so often, relied on, exploited, suffered from, complained about, needed ...

No matter how bad things have gotten in my life, I have always known I could call on my parents' strength.

The first time I was ever away from home for an extended period, I used to call the folks even when I knew they weren't home. I'd let the phone ring, drawing strength just knowing the phone was ringing in their apartment....

Years later, when things were at their worst, I called Mom and Dad and said, *Did you ever feel like just getting on a plane and flying away?* Mom answered simply. *Every day of my life. It just doesn't work that way.* And she was right. She and Dad always stood the course with remarkable strength —strength I always relied on....

And this strength is gone.

Dad is dead and Mom's strength, that vast resource, is finally tapped out. The strength came from shame. The strength gone, now only the shame remains.... All this happens without a hair moving.

When it is over, she nods her head and reaches for a diaper.

-------

After Mom, in a state of shock, has gone to the bed (quickly stripped, lined with garbage bags and remade), I frantically clean what I can of the apartment and cover the rest with newspapers. Then I put on the television and, numb, watch images go by in a trance-like state until I sleep too.

I don't know how long I sleep before I am awakened from a nightmare by a nightmare—strangling calls from the bedroom. *Help! Help me! Help! Oh, dear God, help me!* I run into the room find her in the middle of a coughing/retching/choking spell. She is being hurled about by convulsions and it looks as if her body is trying to tear itself in half. We have been through many of these episodes. They are triggered by tension and, befitting the day, this is by far the worst ever. I sit next to her and have to struggle just to hold her upright. The eyes of this woman who never wants to be helped are full of a terrified appeal for me to *do* something.

I half-carry, half-drag her to the sink in the kitchen where we usually work through these seizures. I am holding her so tightly I am afraid I will bruise her or break a bone. Still, if I loosen the hold, I will drop her since her body is being so violently collapsed and straightened by the dry heaves. She is like a ship breaking up in a high storm.

I try to talk her through, telling her that she will be alright, but this is worse than the worst I have seen, and I don't know that she will be alright.

We are both helpless in the face of this chaos and madness.

And it is at this moment, as she is jerking forward and backward, coughing and gagging wildly, that "the blockage" the nurse could not dislodge, "the blockage" that was the start of this whole nightmare, it is at this moment that the blockage chooses to give way, slowly at first, but then, continuously, massively. The smell is nauseating, but what is worse is the feeling that my mother is actually falling apart in my hands. That she is dissolving before my eyes. And, through her choking and gagging, my mother keeps saying, *I'm sorry, I'm sorry, I'm so sorry....*

———

When the storm finally passes, we stand at the sink in shock. In stillness. In despair. Though the smell is overwhelming and we know we have to go to the bathroom to change the diaper, we are almost afraid to move.

Mom breaks the silence with a half-whisper asking for water. I run the tap to fill a tumbler. She shakes her head and points to the tiny crystal glass she prefers. I dump the big glass, fill the small one, and after a sip of water, *My God, that tastes good,* my mother tells a story.

To my surprise, it is a story I have never heard before and, unlike any story I have ever heard her tell, it is almost shapeless....

Just the bones of a story really, but she tells it well.

Vividly.

For reasons that will become clear, I can retell it only imperfectly here, but I will do the best I can.

It is a very *short* story, but it took a *very* long time to tell, since Mom had to catch her breath after each thought.

> *You know Mrs. Gilmartin?*

I told her I didn't. And then stood very still as she told her story with absolute concentration between sips of water and long pauses to gather breath.

> *You do. Her husband was my brother's godfather...*
> *Well, he died.*

> *When the oldest son came home from the war...*
> *the mother was...*

> *Sick.*
> *Oh, she was sick.*
> *Terrible sick.*
> *She couldn't care for herself. Well—*
> *The son took her into the bathroom and gave her her bath.*
> *She never got over that.*

The story was so completely unlike my mother's other stories that, at first, I didn't understand it.

It was told so simply, so factually, I couldn't even get a hold of the tone. I had to ask, *What do you mean she never got over that? In a good way or a bad way?* And she said, with conviction —

*Oh, very, very good.*

———

As we stood there in the kitchen, by the sink, surrounded by terrible odor, the shipwreck was suddenly over. The madness ended. An almost impersonal calm descended on us....

My mother had told a story...

And the story worked.

It is an awkward story, but it worked.

And this story conveyed on our shame meaning.

———

To tell this story, my mother had to do several very brave things.

For a moment, she put aside her lifelong story of hard work and survival.

For a moment, she put aside her strength.

For a moment, she even put aside her leading role in her own life story.

And she told a story about being bathed.

An awkward story...a story about a mother and son breaking taboos, reversing roles...an embarrassing story....

But, told without a trace of embarrassment, it becomes a story about kindness—kindness given and kindness received.

In it, weakness, so long feared, is no longer a weakness, but a generous invitation to generosity.

Not much of a story, just the bones of a story really, but it comforted us.

We were terribly alone and embarrassed and ashamed and this fragment of a story comforted us.

It said you are not alone.

No, you are not alone.

In this smell.

In this kitchen.

Even in your loneliness, you are not alone.

Other people have been here.

Other people have been this lonely.

This dirty.

This shamed.

This helpless.

And though they have been all of these things, they have not been foolish.

No, not foolish at all.

In fact, they have been generous and kind to one another.

In fact, though they have been dead for years and their story, in all probability, untold for decades, they are kind and generous to one another still...in this story.

And they are kind to us, too.

Very kind.

For they have left us their story to comfort us in this comfortless moment by the sink in the kitchen.

Not much of a story.

Still, I choose to save this story.

———

Mom is in and out of the hospital emergency room in the next couple of days for purges and cleansings and, bit by bit, some of her strength begins to return. Thanks to her niece Mary Lou, one of Neil's daughters, we find less cumbersome disposable undergarments. Mom begins to figure out how to change them herself.

Though we do not talk about the story again, I can see it working in her.

She no longer apologizes for her situation...for needing help...for asking for it....

She is growing softer...She is growing gentler...Most important of all, she is growing....

Incontestably, she is growing. Growing in a way she could not have grown when she was young.

And that, perhaps, is why we grow old.

Perhaps it is necessary, finally, to return to where the story started. To the initial wound. To the moment our world fell apart for the first time. When we felt that the love available to us wasn't going to be enough. To the place where the initial blockage was...

Maybe we need to a second chance at the stage of the diaper...the walking and falling...the crying from bed for help, only this time conscious, aware, able—if we're lucky—to undo, redo, remake the experience into something better....

To find a better story...

———

## JUNE 26

The end is near.

This morning I got out the tape recorder and told Mom there was a story she told me I'd like to tape.

She said, *What story?* I said, *The story about the soldier.* She says, *What soldier?* And I remind her of the story. *Neil's godfather's wife, Mrs. Gilmartin. You know. You know the story.*

And she asks to be reminded further....

So I tell her the story and she is clearly touched by it. And she thinks and then says, *Billy, I couldn't have told you that story. I've never heard it before in my life.*

Silence.

I insist that she remember.

She can't.

Puzzled, I put away the tape recorder.

She is quiet and thoughtful all day and that night, as she is going to bed, she says, *I'm sorry to disappoint you, Billy. I can tell how much that story means to you, but I really don't know it.*

She has never heard the story.

So the story is only ever told once.

Until now.

### Chapter 14. What's the Point of the Bible?

*Not, I'll not, carrion comfort, Despair, not feast on thee;*
*Not untwist—slack they may be—these last strands of man*
*In me ór, most weary, cry I can no more. I can;*
*Can something, hope, wish day come, not choose not to be.*
*—Gerard Manley Hopkins*

I am urging people to save their stories.

Why?

Because the stories that we have saved, save us.

In the most impossible times, we look back into the Bible and see how many times everything was equally hopeless.

People backed up against the sea manage to walk through it.

Whether it was a miracle or a natural occurrence, still—

Even faced with the last journey of death, Jesus finds hope where others would find only despair.

We know this from the stories that have been saved.

And perhaps, in your saved story, people who come after you will look and say—Yes, at their worst, they still survived.

And perhaps even survived with grace and with generosity.

As I am sure you have.

# 15

# *The Stations in the Ordinary Death of an Ordinary Woman*

**MAY 27–JULY 23**

I did not, as I had vowed, finish this book of memories within a year of my mother's death.

A vow broken.

The movie I was writing while I was looking after her was successful and led to a string of writing jobs which, in turn, led me away from finishing this story. I am taking time to finish it now because if I don't finish it soon I am afraid it will be too late.

During the intervening five years, I've kicked myself when I remembered times I could have been more patient with Mom, more available. Friends assure me I did fine, but they weren't there when tempers flared, when patience wore out, or when I simply disappeared. I could have done better. It makes me sad to think that. Maybe that's why I haven't finished this book. It is certainly the reason I haven't listened to the tapes. . . .

The tapes I made of my mother (one just four days before she died) have been sitting in my desk drawer since she died. Wondering if they would make me sad, I listened to them this morning and heard my mother's voice for the first time in five years.

As she speaks, through shortness of breath, tiredness, and sometimes terrible pain (I know Jesus had a rough time dying, but I'll put nine months of cancer up against one Good Friday any day), I find I have a new regret. A good friend, Mary Merrill, told me shortly after Mom's death that there would be a lot of things I would regret not having asked my parents, but, based on the tapes, I asked everything I wanted to know. *My boyfriends before Pete? Oh, you don't want to hear about them, Billy!* Her sex life with Dad? *There was never any problem there, Billy!* After listening to the tapes (and laughing through most of them), what I regret isn't something I didn't ask her, but something I didn't tell her.

And I could have.

At one point it was right on the tip of my tongue.

But I didn't.

So, for what it's worth, I'll tell her now.

And tell you how Mary died and finish this story.

These are the stations in the ordinary death of an ordinary woman.

---

### Mary Falls for the First Time
**MAY 27**

*Billy, get up.*

6:45 a.m.

It's not that I don't hear her.

*Bill ... Bill ...*

*Billy, get up.*

Ladylike. Soft. I hear her and I answer as I have from early childhood—*I'm up*—and I roll over and bury myself deeper in the blankets.

*Billy, Billy, get up....*

My mother and father spent every morning of the first seventeen years of my life trying to get me out of bed. When all else failed, Dad would sprinkle water on me and, mad as a cartoon character, I would leap out of bed (which is all he wanted) and chase him (short chase, small apartment) threatening murder (he'd lock himself in the bathroom and laugh) not because he sprinkled water on me but because he *enjoyed* it.

When I was allowed to sleep in on Saturdays, Mom—up early because days off from work were still workdays at home—Mom would strip the bed and remake it while I was still in it while Dad would sing to the tune of "Here We Go 'Round The Mulberry Bush": *Lazy Billy, will you get up? Will you get up? Will you get up? Lazy Billy, will you get up? We need the sheets for the table.*

This morning is no different.

*Bill... Billy... get up.*

I answer, as always, *I'm up*, until I hear—

*I've had a fall....*

I am out of the bed like a shot, looking down the corridor. And there's Mom on the floor, but it doesn't look like she has fallen. On the contrary, she sits on the floor gracefully, looking composed—even posed—as if to have her picture taken on the grass at a picnic or on the beach. But it's not a picnic or a day at the beach. Is it? I'm not very good right out of bed. Who fell? Didn't somebody fall?

*Good morning, Billy,* she says. *Sorry to get you up.* And she smiles, which is further disorienting. It's 6:45 in the morning and Mom is lying on the floor acting like a perfect lady. I ask what happened. *I don't know, Billy. I went to turn on the lamp, and I could feel myself falling, and the next thing I knew I was on the floor. Just stupid, I guess....*

Has she broken anything? Should I call 911? I wonder but do not ask. Neither of us wants to rush into anything, so I sit on the floor with her and we talk.

Because we are both acutely aware that this moment might be a turning point in Mom's dying, our perfectly ordinary morning conversation is heightened with reverence for the possible significance of this moment. *How did you sleep?* Good. You? *Not bad. How late did you work?* Very. *...Did you see anything good on TV?...Did anybody call?...Did you dream?...*

———

Mom and I always talk through our dreams.

Mine are sprawling and baroque which, I think, is one of the reasons I have so much trouble getting up in the morning. But even when they aren't elaborate, they are usually couched in compelling images—

One night I dreamt that my father was a rabbi dancing with the Torah. And I was the Torah.

Mom's dreams are resolutely prosaic.

*Billy, I dreamed I was ironing a very large shirt, the biggest shirt I ever ironed, and now that it's done I don't know where to hang it,* and she laughs. Occasionally she addresses envelopes in her sleep. Not a lot to interpret here. Dad used to dream of running for subways he missed. These are the dreams of hard-working people.

———

After a while on the floor, Mom laughs.

*This is nice*, she says. *We should do this more often.* And, as we laugh, a certain euphoria creeps in. Today's not the day. Mom fell. That's all. Nothing more significant. We won't have to face the unfaceable today. Slowly, very slowly, checking at every stage of the game, I get Mom to her feet.

———

The afternoon of Mom's fall, I go over to Vince's pharmacy.

I buy the cane she had been resisting since the day she kicked the physical therapist across the living room. Now she loves it. She loves the cane and I hate it. To my surprise, I miss the reckless defiance of her wobbling around the apartment on her own power. More carefully now, the journey goes on.

———

*Stupid! Stupid!*

Mary says it with great bitterness and anger.

*Stupid!*

She says it to herself about herself.

*Stupid!*

She has spilled a cup of tea.

As her ability to take care of herself diminishes, *My right eye's all blurry, Billy. How am going to do the checkbook?*, she is redirecting all her anger—that powerful anger that sustained her through a lifetime—against herself. At this point she has no other target. She's made her peace over the years with just about everybody else.

She has spilled a cup of tea.

*Stupid!*

She doesn't get to the phone before it stops ringing.

*Stupid!*

Mary, mocked by the new limitations of her body, becomes enraged with herself.

*Stupid! Stupid! Stupid!*

---

### Water from the Wound
#### JUNE 17

My mother won't talk to me.

She can't.

Her fear has driven her so far within herself that sound won't come out of her any more than light out of a black hole.

She's been on the couch for an hour, paralyzed with fear.

In the past few weeks, Carol, the brilliant, relentless home health nurse that Dr. P has gotten for us, has been dogged in her pursuit of Mom's individual ills and now has her—except for the fact that she is dying—pretty healthy. We've gotten back into crossword puzzles, daily visits from Mom's friends, phone calls, comforting fights between the two of us, and sports until...

Until water started pouring out of Mom's body.

When I noticed on Wednesday that Mom's slippers were wet, I assumed she had stepped in water I'd spilled doing dishes. Thursday when I noticed the couch where she sleeps during the day was damp, I assumed that Barbara, the home health aide, had spilled water while helping Mom clean up. Then, this morning, Mom said, *Look at this!*

*My foot is wet again.* I changed her socks and began to suspect (and dread) another bathroom problem. Then, a half
hour later, on a hunch, I checked her feet again. The fresh
socks were soaked through just as if she had been out walking shoeless in the rain. Soaking sopping wet. Since we both
knew she had been near nothing wet, there was only one
place all this water could be coming from. The water—if
that's what it was—was pouring directly out of her legs.
Lots of it.

This is not the way a living body functions and suddenly terror sets in, this time more deeply than I have ever
seen before.

She will not, cannot speak, and I need her to.

I need her permission to call the doctor because...
well...because it's her life and her foot and her water and
she ought to be able to do as she wants with them. But she
is frightened. Not of the doctor who is a comforting presence. She is afraid because she's in the presence of something over which she has no power at all. She can't iron it or
organize it, or stamp it and mail it, or put in overtime for it,
or even sacrifice her way around it. It is her death and she
is helpless before it.

Finally, after a lot of quiet, false, reassuring talk on my
part, she speaks. She says two words.

*I'm scared.*

And I am deeply grateful. It's a start. We talk. We
don't talk about dying. We talk about going to the hospital. I promise her that she will not go to the hospital and
then I call the doctor to find out if she will.

Only the doctor's not in. He has taken his family away
for the weekend to celebrate their boy's birthday. So I talk
to Chris, the nurse who runs Dr. P's office, and tell her what's
happened, starting with the slippers two days ago....

Mom had met Chris at early visits to Dr. P. I got to like Chris on a visit when, after I asked her why she had a cast on her wrist, she told me she had gotten so mad at home one night, she broke it pounding the wall. I trust Chris for her honesty and the fact that she hit the wall instead of a family member. I got to love her when she forced Mom to take her home number when she found out I was going to be away on a trip. *Now you call me, Mary, if there's any problem at all.* And hearing the symptoms, Chris says,

*Your mother's skin is weeping?*

Skin? Weeping? This sounds like poetry to me, but evidently it's a medical term. Her body is weeping for its own dissolution. Chris says, *Call Dr. B. He's Dr. P's back up.*

I call.

When he asks what's wrong, I start with the wet slippers and he is curt. *I am with a patient. What?* I reduce everything to symptoms: Old woman. Cancer. Legs wet. No discoloration. Swollen ankles. And he is genuinely interested in this. Evidently her body isn't processing protein. I will get a fuller explanation from Dr. P, but the essential piece of information is, *It can wait till Monday.* A reprieve. *Call if there's difficulty breathing, redness in the legs, or fever.* After shouting into the living room, *We're OK*, I report back to Chris and she says, *Good, I was just worried that it would turn into cellulitis, get infected, and you'd have to go to the hospital for IV antibiotics.* I say we need an appointment Monday but I expect that will be difficult because the doctor's been away. And Chris says *Difficult? Not for your mother. She's a good lady. Give her my love.*

As I give a full blow-by-blow to Mom, I can see that she is unclenching some. She has a few days to prepare for whatever is coming and, really, that's all she needs. When I'm done, she asks—out of all the things she could ask

about: her medical condition, the missing doctor, the diagnosis, the prognosis) she asks, *Isn't Chris a lovely nurse? I*
agree. Then, as she unclenches a bit more and asks,

*And she said she likes me?*

And I say, *Very much.*

Mom unclenches. I don't. I announce that I will be hard
to deal with for the rest of the day because this was supposed to be a day when I was going to New York. Mom understands and, as she sleeps that afternoon, I walk up to the
mall, well, because that's the only place to walk to. I buy
several pair of large, inexpensive shoes hoping one will fit
Mom's now swollen feet for the doctor's visit on Monday.
(The largest shoes, as it turns out, are still too small, so we
slit them at the back and bind them with gaffer's tape. Not
bad.)

------

### The Walk Down the Corridor
#### JUNE 17—EVENING

That night, there's such a sense of relief in the house that it
feels like a holiday. Mom, feeling energetic, asks me if I
could help her take a walk around the house.

I like doing this, if she isn't too shaky, because after we
walk through the four rooms of the apartment, she is usually tired out and sleeps well. I excuse myself to go to the
bathroom and, when I get back, I can't find my mother and
it's not that big an apartment.

She is in the closet.

*Mom, what are you doing in the closet?*

When she comes out, she is wearing a jacket and smiling.
Laughing, I ask her what the hell she's doing in a jacket. She

doesn't understand my confusion. She says, *I thought we were going to take a walk around the house.* And it takes me a moment, but I realize that she is expecting to take a walk around the whole apartment complex, a walk she has not been capable since May 23rd—the last time she walked outside.

———

It was a long walk for her even then, but it was a beautiful day and she was really looking forward to it. When we came out the door, the attractive girl from next door was rushing the season, sunbathing, face down, bra untied. Faced with this picture of perfect health and youth, Mom got embarrassed about her own physical condition and wanted to go back inside. Once we got walking, though, we had a very good time. I know the date because I happened to take a picture.

*Mom, you can't walk around the house.*

She says, *Oh that's right. I can't, can I?* And she laughs, amused at having forgotten something so basic. I ask, *Did you forget you were sick?* She laughs again and says, *I forgot I was old.* It was a sort of masterpiece of forgetting.

Shaking her head at her own foolishness, she puts the jacket back and says, *Can we still take a walk?* I say *Sure.* And she says, *Let's walk to the front door.* And we do.

Holding her cane in one hand and putting her other through my arm, she walks out the door of our apartment and we walk down the red-rugged corridor to the front door.

She sets the pace and the tone. We walk slowly and in silence. Carefully. More than carefully, we walk ceremonially …as if walking past a reviewing stand. Or in a turn-of-the-century Easter Parade. She is walking as if this walk were important somehow and is being observed and approved of. Something is happening that I am not in on, but I walk quietly and try to stay with Mom's ceremonial pace.

Mom gives an occasional Queen-of-England-like wave. Which puzzles me. I ask, *Who are you waving to?* With a smile she answers, *I don't know.* And waves again.

At our furthest point, the front door, we open the door and enjoy the spring night air in silence. Then Mom says something very odd.

Silence.

Then—

She says with conviction, *I want to get my shoes on and walk around the house with you.*

Silence.

Though she clearly means the impossible walk around the apartment complex, she is not now forgetful of where she is or her age or her sickness or the fact that she is dying. Not at all. But, standing in the fresh air of the spring night, this endlessly practical lady says with great assurance of that impossible walk, *Yes, I look forward to that day.*

The speech is over.

Two sentences.

And we walk back slowly, with an occasional wave, reviewing the troops or whatever it is that we have been doing.

When we get back inside, my mother thanks me quite formally for the walk and asks for help to get to bed. The fifteen-yard walk has worn her out.

And I stay up that night wondering: Why do I so want to get away? What play in New York, what movie, what work of art could possibly be better than watching this old woman discover she's looking forward to something that can never happen—looking forward freely, joyously, anticipating without even the slightest regret something that can never happen. The generosity of that staggers me. If I could live as well as she is dying, what couldn't I do?

———

Monday we go to the doctor. Chris greets her with a hug and they talk. *Mary, I was so worried about you....*

Mom and I go in to see the doctor and Dr. P explains medically what happened. The liver isn't letting liquid return to the heart and after the explanation Mom asks, *How was your boy's birthday?* And the doctor brightens right up. *Great. Just great.* And you can see he means it. *We all went to a water slide park. Have you ever been to a water park, Mary? You have to go sometime.*

Mom agrees to go.

———

### The Agony in the Doctor's Office
#### JULY 21

July 21st was our last visit to the doctor.

Of course we didn't know that.

If we had, we would have brought a camera and presents. Instead, we just brought Mom. And that was hard enough.

It's been harder and harder for Mom to get around unassisted. Not often, but some days, I have to accompany her from the time she gets up until she goes to bed....

The first night I had to help her get to bed—she had stayed up late watching the Knicks beat the Pacers—I saw part of her good night ritual I had never seen before. After she had said her prayers and her good nights to pictures of family and friends, Jesus on the wall, the statue of St. Francis, and a few stuffed animals, she walked into her bedroom, tossed her bathrobe on a chair, and shuffled over to her desk where her papers are piled high. For her last act of the night, she reached behind the unanswered correspondence and the bills that were piled up there and picked up a picture of her and Dad I hadn't seen before.

*Pete and Mary are at a party, dressed in their best. Dad is looking like it's a three-scotch-night, but Mom isn't disapproving. No. Instead, both their heads are thrown back in laughter.*

She says to the picture, *Good night, Pete,* kisses the picture, gets into bed, and is asleep as soon as her head hits the pillow.

Before I leave, I take a good look at the picture. My father's face, though still visible, has been almost worn away with years of kisses.

I am up before her this morning to get her ready for the doctor, but I'm up before her most mornings now. Both of us wake up tired, since we are up every hour or so through the night for the pain or the bathroom, *Go to bed, Billy, I can do this myself.* We're punch-drunk and can no longer tell day from night. This morning, when Connie, the neighborhood mystic, and her couldn't-be-more-down-to-earth husband Bill arrive to drive us the doctor, Mom is in pain, so I give her her morphine early. Very early. So be it. Otherwise, she'll never make it. *Billy, I can't do this anymore. I can't. I just can't.* She's been saying this for months, but getting her down the stairs to the car, Connie on one side, me on the other, it feels true. We are practically carrying her and the pain is so intense she can't speak.

The alternative?

Hospice.

Hospice means six months to live. The doctor, who says it could be years, is scheduling a CT scan to check on the progression of the disease. But we aren't thinking in years now. Or months or weeks or days or hours or minutes. We are thinking in steps. Steps to the car. One foot in front of the other. *Terrible, terrible,* she says.

We pull up to the doctor's side entrance.

The side entrance bypasses the waiting room, saving precious steps. Mom greets Melanie (Chris isn't here today) wordlessly, with a nod. Melanie, who can see we are in trouble, drops everything and rushes to help. Trying to save more steps, she says, *Mary, let's get your weight before you go in to the examining room,* and Mom, doing her best to comply, steps up on the scale. There is no *How's your school going, Melanie?* today. Mom is just trying to hang on. Melanie adjusts the weights quickly and is genuinely pleased. *Mary, you've gained two pounds. You're up to 97 again. Isn't that great?* And Mary smiles, nods, and says, with a smile, *"Butter."* As she tries to step off the scale, she abruptly bends from the waist, then involuntarily bolts straight up like she's been shot by a sniper and suddenly half-steps/half-falls off the scale. I grab her as she grabs a wall. The nurse grabs her other arm to help. Mom, needing freedom of movement to do what she's about to do, shakes her off, trying to explain with a look that she appreciates the offered help. And I think, *Oh, shit. What are we going to do now?* We are in for a bad hour, hour and a half, a bad pain episode where she can't sit, stand, or lay down with any comfort, so she lurches from one position to another in a frantic whiplash set of motions. Which is what she is doing now. Mary Cain, who tries always to be the perfect lady, is bouncing off the walls of the doctor's office. Literally. Holding on to one wall. Pushing off. Grabbing another. I hold her up and accompany her as I do at home, but this isn't home where we have our emergency routines down pat. We are in the doctor's office, and these people have their own routines. The startled nurse says, *I'll get the doctor. You won't have to wait, Mary,* and runs out of the office.

And we wait.

And we walk and lurch and grab and struggle.

Melanie returns and tries to get Mom up on the examining table so she can lie down and rest. I know this isn't going to work, but Melanie needs to do something and Mom is trying to please, so she steps on the little foot stool attached to the table, turns, sits, tries to lie back and— bam!—lurches off the table. We catch her and she finds some comfort resting her head against the wall.

In the quiet that follows, Mom asks Melanie, *What happens when a patient can't come to see the doctor anymore?* and Melanie says, *There are some patients the doctor goes to see.* This, though not a promise, is a good answer. Mom nods and we don't say more.

Dr. P arrives.

He has clearly been alerted to the situation and he rushes in. *Mary, how are you?* Mom is panting like a fighter in a late round. *Doctor, I'm near out of my mind.* The doctor, genuinely sympathetic, says, *I know, Mary, I know,* puts on his stethoscope and goes to listen to Mom's heart. But the second the stethoscope touches her chest, she lurches away, apologizing as she does. She starts to run around the room, bending and straightening. As Mom tries to find a position of comfort, the doctor watches. As Mom continues to move about the room, he looks to me. Back to her. He asks the usual questions. Tries to stick to the usual routine.

And as she moves from unsatisfactory position to unsatisfactory position, Mary tells him, *Things aren't too bad, Doctor. The ankles are down,* and he says, *I wonder what caused that.* And Mom, on the verge of tears, pounding the wall, says, *Oh God . . . oh God . . . oh my God . . . what am I going to do?*

Nobody answers.

Nobody knows what to say.

The usual routine of the doctor's office has been broken. Dr. P can't examine her. Mom can't take out her index cards and discuss her medications. We are in the presence of sheer physical pain. A tour de force of pain.

She bends and straightens and bends and straightens, saying, *Oh dear, oh dear, oh, dear and I'm so sorry, Doctor.*

The doctor, who is a tall man, suddenly does a very surprising thing.

Suddenly he sits.

He sits on a very low stool.

Not even a stool.

Lower than a stool.

He sits on the step of the examining table and he puts his head into his hands and I begin to realize that he can't deal with pain. And I think, *We should have done this a long, long time ago.* Have we hidden this pain from him by being social and pulled-together on our visits? But he is seeing the pain now, understanding what we have been talking about. He's seeing it and he looks so lost.

Very lost.

And very, very young.

And I think—this might be the reason he became a doctor.

Because he can't bear pain.

It's a good reason to become a doctor actually. He made a good choice, becoming a doctor. Then he looks up and asks me a very odd question. *Can I give her more pain medication?*

The doctor asks *me*, not the reverse.

And I want to cry.

I want to cry because I know we will never come here again. There is no reason to. Sitting there on the stool, he is already no longer her doctor. He's just a very young man, feeling terrible because there is nothing he can do to help Mary Cain, one of his first patients.

This is our last visit.

The first of many lasts.

And that's a relief, but it's also very, very sad. The doctor's office has been so important, such a place of hope. Things get written on slips of paper here and you take the paper to Vince at the pharmacy, *How's your mother today?*, and he gives you something in a bottle, *Make sure you take it for the full ten days* or *This can be crushed and put in applesauce* or *There's one refill on this one*, and you're better. At least a little better. For a while. Until . . . but now there aren't even any more untils. No more doctor. No more hope.

Mary has finally settled in a position of comfort.

The room is quiet again.

The doctor says he will make the call for hospice. And he's canceling next week's CT scan because it's clear that she can't go through with it. *Oh, thank you, Doctor,* says Mary. *I was so frightened of that. I was so scared.*

And the visit gets very fast after that. The doctor leaves and it's time for Mary to leave. She is in very bad pain, but she won't take the side door out. She insists on going to the front desk to say goodbye to the girls. It's not a very satisfying goodbye, even though Laurie hugs her with genuine warmth. Mom's beloved Chris isn't there, and Mom will never see her again. (Chris will see Mom again. At the wake.) I wish I had my camera to take a picture. Something to hold onto. But that's the point, I suppose. There is nothing more to hold onto.

In the car on the way home Connie asks, *What happened?* and I say, *I can't tell you.* Silence. Then—*I mean, it isn't classified information but if I start to tell you I will cry and that's probably not helpful right now.* And Bill jumps right in and talks about their grown daughter's softball game last night, one of Mom's favorite topics, and Mom smiles politely as she tries to follow the conversation while pushing back hard against the car seat trying to control her pain. We are all in pain. Connie, who has tremendous feeling for Mary, keeps saying, *We'll be home in no time, Mary. Hang on.*

And I know what she is thinking.

------

During the visit, the doctor, helpless, said, *Well, it's clear that you can't come to the office any more.*

Mom nodded.

In a strange way this was good news. She won't have to make this trip anymore. Then she asks, certain of what the answer will be (it's less a question than a cue), *Will you come to see me, Doctor?*

And the doctor doesn't say anything.

Silence.

We all wait for his answer.

Then he says, *We'll arrange for care,* which, though a fine answer, is definitely the wrong answer. This young sympathetic doctor is cutting her loose.

The doctor says, *I won't leave you alone, Mary....* but she's alone already and we all know it.

------

Finally back in the apartment by ourselves, we are silent, which is odd for us. Silent, worn out, and utterly blank. Mom, after another dose of morphine, is out cold.

Paulette calls, furious that Mom had to go to the doctor. I tell her that it was the last visit. She is much relieved. Hospice. *Well, finally.* But she can hear how depressed I am and says, *I'll be right down.*

When Paulette arrives, she announces she is staying for the afternoon, shoves ten dollars in my pocket and tells me to go see a movie. The next thing I know I am out of the apartment and on my way to the mall thinking, *I hope to God I get old like Paulette.*

It's a long, uphill walk to the mall and, walking by the side of the road (no sidewalks) with cars and trucks zooming by, I find myself sobbing. I tell myself there will be a time and a place to cry, but it is probably not now and definitely not at the mall. I pull myself together at the mall and go to see a thriller. That seems a safe bet. At the end of the movie, a character going into the witness protection program says to a friend, *I'll never see you again, will I?* and I begin to sob. Not polite tears, but big, mucousy sobs. The lights come up and the ushers look at me oddly—and I don't blame them because, trust me, I am the only human being ever to cry at this movie.

On the way back home, I talk out loud to my sorrow and I say, *Look, grief, I promise you, I promise that I will not ignore you. I will take time and let you do whatever you want. I just have to find the right place and the right time. When I get home there are things to be done. Leave me free to do them.* And I try to think of something that isn't sad. But I can't. So I think, *Well, then, just put one foot in front of the other and walk,* and even that reminds me of my parents and I cry harder. I do not want to cry.

So I think about work, the writing I am supposed to be doing, and the tears clear up. And I wonder if finally that's all my work is—a way to avoid crying. And I think of Pat Tampone, an accomplished technical director at a theater I directed. She was a tremendous worker, a beautiful woman, a good friend, and she cried about something every day. One day when I asked her, *How do you manage to cry every day?* She asked me back, *How do you manage not to?*

————

The apartment is dark when I arrive home.

Not a single light on.

I panic.

What the hell happened?

Paulette, reading by the fading sunlight of a window, says, *Nothing's wrong. I just don't want to give Niagara Mohawk one penny more than I have to!*

I tell Paulette I was crying during the movie, and she says, *Well, it's dark in there. Nobody probably saw you.* Mom wakes up. *Billy, is that you?* She says goodbye to Paulette and Paulette, as always, leaves without accepting thanks of any kind. *Don't be silly, Billy. What was I doing anyway?*

————

The day is badly bruised and we do our best to get through it. Pain management. Dinner. Mom sleeps on the couch in front of a Mets game and I go to the back room to write and everything seems tired, sad, and pointless. I can't write and I can't read and I can't even think, so I say, *OK, sorrow, now's your chance.*

And I cry.

Freely and heavily.

About everything.

About the pain and about the fact that the pain will be over soon.

I cry because this is so hard and because it's going to end.

I cry because she's my mother and because, mother or not, we've been through so much together in the past year and have become such good friends.

I cry about everything and its opposite. I stop short of howling, but only barely, and I think, *What is the USE of this!!* There are things to be done. And I pull myself together and go into the kitchen to fix Mom's medication.

Mom gets up from the couch and gets ready for bed. *I can do this myself tonight, Billy. You get the pills ready,* and as I do, I get crying again. And I know that this time, I am not going to be able to stop.

Mom is in the bedroom sitting on the edge of her bed. She is glum. She has been glum all night. I go in and sit next to her and I cry. It's the first time I have cried in her presence since this whole ordeal started. It's quiet crying and Mom doesn't say anything. Neither do I. I can't. Besides, what's to say? Well, maybe this. I say,

*Mom, I've been crying all night.*

She nods. Then I say,

*I'm sorry that you're so sick.*

And I cry quietly, unstoppably.

She says, quietly and simply, *I know you are. I know you care so much. . . .*

*Well,* she adds, *there's nothing I can do about it. I've tried to be pleasing my whole life. Sometimes I've succeeded. That's the way it is. . . .*

And I ask, *Do you cry?*

*All the time,* she says. *Inside.*

*What makes you cry?*
*Only the good things.*
And we sit for a while. Then she says,
*I'm so tired,* and she puts her head on my shoulder and we sit for a while longer.
Then she says, *Well, time for bed.*
And she gets up.
She goes into the bathroom to take care of her hair and I get her morphine ready and when she comes into the kitchen we start to work on the morning's unfinished crossword. *There's a lot to do,* she says, since we didn't even begin the puzzles this morning. *Well, let's get busy.*
And the mood lightens.
Not just a little.
The sorrow lifts entirely.
We work on the puzzle and we laugh and we talk and we stay up very late. Once we finish the crossword, *There! All done! Give me an A on that!* we start on the Jumble. It is almost like a party. And we are very aware of what a good time we are having...and I think, *Well, maybe that's it. Maybe that's what she needed. She needed somebody to cry for her. She needed someone to mourn. And maybe that's the use of sorrow.*
And we stay up as late as we can. *You know what I think that Jumble word is? Modern! See, that's it! Modern!*

———

## Mary Dies
### JULY 23

She's sleeping well and I feel terrible that I have to wake her.
*Mom...Mom...Get up...You have to get up...*

I hate disturbing good pain-free sleep. But I shake her. *Mom...Mom...* And, as she looks at me drowsily. *The nurse got here early. You have to get up.* And Mom says, *But she's not supposed to come till later.* And I say, *I know. She's early. Something about her car. Somebody had to drop her off, so we're her first stop. She's here. You have to get up.* And Mom, who used to leap out of bed, says, *Billy, I don't know if I can.*

But she tries.

The way I get Mom up these days is I cross my arms at the wrists, she grabs hold of my forearms, I pull and she sits up. We try this, but she doesn't have enough strength to hold on and she falls back onto the bed. Sometimes she laughs when this happens, but this time she doesn't. She just lies there. I go to try again, but she gestures that she wants a second. She just lies there. And I wonder if this is the fall she's not going to get up from.

*Can you make it?*

Mom is thinking.

I think we don't have time for this. The nurse is waiting. But Mom will not be rushed this morning. She's working something out. Whatever it is, it's more important than keeping the nurse waiting, and for Mom there has never been anything more important than that.

Then she speaks simply and with great clarity.

She says objectively, almost as if she is speaking of someone else, someone for whom she cares a great deal, *I'm a very sick girl, Billy.*

*I know,* I say.

And she thinks and says,

*I wish I'd get better...*

*I know.*

There is a pause and then she says simply, *Well...it's not going to happen.*

I say nothing.

This is said just as a fact.

Acknowledgement is not necessary.

Then she says a remarkable thing. Also as a fact. Very, very simple.

*And that's alright too.*

My one regret is what I didn't say to you at that moment. So I'll say it now, Mom.

Mom, we talked a lot in the months that you were so sick. Nothing went unsaid. But I wish at this moment, the moment you said it was alright that you weren't going to get better, I wish I had said something to you. I wish I had said I was proud of you. Because I was. I was very proud of you. It was something you'd been working on for a long time, step by painful step, but you got there. No bitterness. No regrets. No unfulfilled yearnings. It was all alright. I know there were a few things you were unhappy about (the only stat the Mets were leading the league in was being hit by pitched balls), but that would have to be alright too.

I'm glad it was alright.

And I just want to tell you that I think you did well, in spite of what you thought about yourself at the time. You did well at this dying thing. Because that's what you really did that morning. You'd be around for another week or so, but the dying part was done. Death was alright. There was nothing more to fear. Nothing more to sweat blood about. The work was done. The biology would have to catch up when it could. You did well. You didn't get the closets cleaned, but you did manage to look at your own death and say, *And that's alright too.* And I think that's really good. *That's alright too.*

You would go to the doctor no more. And that would be alright. You'd be in pain, but that would be alright. The world would go on without you, and that would be alright. I think that's splendid and I wish I had told you.

I could have, you know. I knew all of this the instant you said, *And that's alright too.* I was full of admiration for you but I was very, very, very, very tired.

But I knew it at the time.

Then you said *Now get me up, Billy* and I did—and it was hard because we were both so tired. After you did get up, I sat on your bed, impressed as hell with you. I listened as you scuffled out into the living room and I heard you, bone-tired, say (and mean) to the nurse, *Oh, Debbie, it's you. Billy didn't tell me it was you! Don't you look lovely this morning! What's wrong with the car?...*

I think you did well.

I know you always hoped that you'd die like your mother, passing in your sleep. But I'm glad you didn't. I know it was very, very hard work, dying the way you did. You never did anything the easy way. And you did this—like all the other hard work of your life—very, very well.

And I'll never get to tell you this because, unlike Dad, you're not coming back to visit. No need to. There is nothing left undone. Not the closets, you didn't get to the closets, but you got the loose ends of life closed up. You've done the work. All that work. You've done it now. And it's alright. So, congratulations, Mom. You did well. I'm proud of you.

And I know you'll never get this message, but you know what?

That's alright too.

———

Mom changed after this; I did not.

It's hard to describe the change exactly, but perhaps this story will give you an idea.

I had just bought a new CD and was playing it loud while trying to complete a rewrite. When I came out of my room and passed Mom's bedroom, I saw her twitching on the bed. I ran in thinking she was having a seizure of some sort and blaming myself for missing the trouble signs by playing the music too loud.

I ran in and said, *Mom, Mom, what's wrong?*

She looked puzzled and said, *What do you mean?*

I said, *You're shaking on the bed.*

She looked at me like I was losing my mind and said, *I was keeping time with the music. It's such beautiful music....*

––––––

Her dreams changed after this point too.

No more ironing shirts or addressing envelopes.

*Billy, I've been climbing and climbing and it's the damndest thing, I can't get my leg over the rock at the top of the mountain. I'm so tired, Billy.*

Or—

*I had the oddest dream. I dreamed that Sister Honora* (a family friend) *was in the Holy Land* (she was) *and she was walking through Jerusalem praying for me....*

Or, best of all, her last dream. At least the last one I knew about.

Two days before her death, Mom was smiling in her sleep during a nap. When she woke up I told her she'd been smiling and asked what she had been dreaming about. She thought carefully, then she smiled again.

I said, *What?*

She said, *Willie Mays.*

And she laughed.

*I've been dreaming about Willie Mays. I was at Shea Stadium and I was watching Willie Mays make this amazing catch....*

Then she raised her hand as if to salute him and said with a smile, *Say hey, Willie!*

———

So, as always, you did the hard thing well. So now relax. Don't climb the mountain anymore. No need. You're at the top. Sit down and enjoy the view. Can you see Jerusalem from there? What does it look like? Does it shine?

And, please, if you and Dad ever run across Willie Mays, please say *Hey!* for me.

*Chapter 15.*
**Stations in the Ordinary Death of an Ordinary Woman**

*"Where you go I will go, and where you stay I will stay. Your people will be my people and your God my God. Where you die I will die, and there I will be buried. May the Lord deal with me, be it ever so severely, if even death separates you and me."*
                                                              —*Ruth 1:16–17*

It is possible that the book of Ruth is the most beautiful book in the bible.

It is a simple story, really.

And the landmark quote from the book is cited above. "Where you go, I will go and where you stay, I will stay. Even death will not separate us."

There is great beauty in that.

And that is what the Stations are about.

Sometimes—often—the emphasis is put on the terrible pain, but I don't think, finally, that's what the Stations of the Cross are about.

I think they are about keeping company with someone who is on a last journey.

If you stay the course, perhaps you can be of help when someone falls. Most of the stations are made up of falling. Wipe a face. Carry a burden.

It takes some courage not to run when there is nothing left to do.

But—as with Ruth—there is beauty in the staying.

## *16*

# *How to Write a New Book for the Bible*

After my mother died, I decided to write a new book for the Bible to honor my parents. I vowed I would write this book—The Book of Cain—in the calendar year after I cleaned out their apartment, leaving it empty of any sign they had ever lived.

In that first year, I wrote all the big events in the small story of my family's life. Five years later, I wrote the details of my mother's last weeks. Now, five years later, ten years after locking their apartment door and returning the key, there is only one small detail left to write and still I hesitate, tempted to write—as I have done for years—work that means much less to me.

Why?

Maybe because it *is* a small thing—so small it went unnoticed by almost everyone at the time.

Or maybe... maybe it's just hard to believe that the final small detail is worth telling.

And yet, from a biblical perspective, it's probably the one element that matters, the essence of revelation, the reason to write a new book of the Bible in the first place. Still, so small as to go unnoticed?

Well—I will try.

———

Since my story particularly deals with mothers, I will add a rule that applies specifically to this story:

Mothers in the Bible are not sweet, well-behaved people.

Mothers in the Bible know that God's ways are not their ways and, worthy daughters of Eve, they generally prefer their ways.

Sarah laughs at God. Rebecca steals Esau's birthright for her favorite, Jacob. Moses's mother is willing to pretend not to be his mother so she can mother him.

Even Jesus's mother, Mary—though she's painted as meek and compliant in later telling of the story—definitely fits the biblical mother profile. She pressures her son into performing a miracle before he's ready. Then, once his miracles build him a following, she's not shy about sending the relatives to try and get him to stop doing them and come home. Even though he was a grown man and God, she thought she knew better and tried to arrange his life for him.

Mary wasn't weak and compliant.

Mary was a mother.

————

My mother—one quiet morning in July, toward the very end of her life—was shocked at an obituary in the morning paper.

Mom's hairdresser Gloria, had lost her husband to a completely unexpected heart attack. Mom loved Gloria and was heartbroken over her loss. And a little angry. She was old and increasingly ready to die. Why in the world should Gloria's husband—a young man—be dying and not her?

There's not a lot you can do in the face of death, but Mom would do what she could.

She added "Write Gloria" to her to-do list.

And my mother got that sympathy card out to Gloria, and all other birthday and anniversary cards. In fact, though nobody believed her young doctor who said she might live for years, getting Christmas cards out this year seemed, in mid-July, like a possibility. In fact, I had started buying Christmas presents for Mom to give her friends, though, if she didn't feel she could make it to Christmas, we agreed she would give them ahead of time. Still, Christmas seemed like a definite possibility.

And, strangely, ever since Mom had decided recently that dying was perfectly alright, there had been a sense of continuing holiday in the house. We are told that there are five stages of dying, the last one being acceptance. Once Mom got there, our worry about how-much-time-Mom-had-left was replaced with a topsy-turvy sense of having all the time in the world. We were a bit disoriented because pain management kept us up most nights, but even that seemed alright. There was something pleasant about doing the crossword together in the middle of the night.

We still had our battles, of course. Mom had recently asked me to take over her checkbook. She had scared herself by writing a $1230 check for a $123 bill. Since Mom's bookkeeping had always been a source of pride for her, I promised to check her math, but insisted that she keep writing her own checks. *OK, Billy, just don't shout at me.*

After any number of these small battles, she suggested —and this was *very* unusual—that I take a short break and go to New York. I assumed what she really meant was that she wanted a break from me. I didn't care about the reason. Any chance I could get out of Syracuse, I took.

Mom, though sharp mentally, now needed someone in the house pretty much around the clock, so I called my brother Paul to ask him to come up from El Paso for a few days. Though it was short notice, we got the tickets arranged and Paul hopped on a plane.

———

When my brother arrived, he and my mother were shy around one another. Delicate might be a better word. Or tender.

My brother was being careful because, called home suddenly, he was looking for some sign of a medical crisis. Mom, not in crisis, was looking for signs of resentment in Paul for being asked to make the trip when there was no crisis.

(And, though we didn't talk about it, there may have still been bruises from the trip Paul had made home when Dad was dying. That trip was the occasion of a huge and mutually lacerating fight between Paul and Mom that led to Dad's last request to Mom—*Take care of Paul.* In any case, by the time Paul returned for Dad's funeral—he hadn't been there for his death—all was well.)

Once Paul realized that Mom was fine and Mom realized that Paul was happy to have the excuse to come, we settled down to catching up.

Mom asked after her granddaughter and daughter-in-law and then—as if it were another family member—her beloved car, which she had given Paul when she realized that she wasn't going to be driving anymore. Nancy, Janet—and the car—were all fine, which delighted Mom. Paul was delighted to announce that his academic team had just won its third straight city championship. And I was delighted because the following morning I'd be on a train for New York City.

It was a good night for all of us.

As a family, we have always been good talkers around the kitchen table and that night we sat and ate and talked and talked and talked... and, even though we were all very tired, nobody wanted to go to bed.

———

The rest of the night was not as easy. Mom was up every hour and a half with serious pain. As always, I got up each time I heard the shuffling of her slippers, but each time I waited a minute longer than usual hoping that Paul would get up—an unfair expectation, since Paul needed his rest if he was going to be doing this himself for the next few nights. So, every hour and a half or so, I went to Mom. I held her, comforted her, encouraged her as she, on her part, kept telling me, *Go to bed, Billy. I'm fine. Go to bed.* But that was interspersed with, *Oh, Billy, what am I going to do? I'm losing my mind!* As usual, we got through it and, by morning, after a few hours of peaceful sleep, the picnic-like mood of the previous night settled in over breakfast.

I review all Mom's medications with Paul—not only what to take and when, but also what goes in what. The morphine, for instance, goes in the applesauce. Each of Mom's medications (except the smallest pills which she can take without food) goes into something and, over the past months, by trial and error, we have become experts on matching medications to food, so that Mom can get her many pills down. The Benadryl goes in the prune juice. The Darvocet goes in the mashed turnips. And on and on. Paul makes notes on all this.

Mom makes her list for the day, including what the three of us have to review when I return—bank statements, insurance documents, etc. I pack and Paul gets ready to drive me to the train station.

As we leave, Mom walks to the door and shouts after me, *Give my love to everybody in New York.*

––––––––

That night, when I return from having dinner with friends in New York, I find two urgent messages from Paul.

I call immediately.

Paul picks up the phone on the first ring and says, *Mom died. I don't know what else to say, Bill. Mom died.*

––––––––

Mom's wake was more crowded than either my brother or I would have imagined.

We had thought, because Mom was old, there would be very few people there. And then, when the place filled up for the afternoon session, we thought the evening wake would be empty. On the contrary. Friends had flown in from New York, Boston, San Francisco. Many of the nurses and aides who had taken such good care of Mom came. And, of course, there were Mom's friends. (I gave them the presents we had been saving for Christmas—Waterford crystal hearts with the words Mom wanted to go with them—*I love you with all my heart.*) I was surprised at the number of people at the wake I didn't know, especially after having spent the last year with her. *I knew your mother in school,* one would say. And another, *You don't know me, but I used to sit next to your mother at church. I loved your mother.* And on and on. *She looked so beautiful in the picture in the paper. What a beautiful woman.*

Gloria the hairdresser came.

When she arrived, she stood at the door for a long moment, looking lost and a bit unsteady on her feet. I went over to her and thanked her for coming. *This is the first time I've come out since my husband died,* she said quietly. I could see that being back in a funeral home was opening wounds for her. I said, *I'll walk up with you if you like.* I gave her my arm for support and we walked to the open casket together. As we stood there, I could sense Gloria becoming deeply quiet. I assumed she was praying for Mom and for her own husband. As the quiet went on, I stole a quick look at Gloria to see if she was alright. She was. In fact, her eyes were perfectly clear. Not a sign of a tear. Gloria was absolutely focused.

She was looking at my mother's hair.

Evaluating it.

Then she said, coolly and professionally, appreciatively, *Not bad.*

———

And Mom did look good.

Paulette, her best friend, had seen to that.

Two days before, Paulette had torn through Mom's closet looking for a knit dress she was sure was there—*a beautiful thing and she never wore it. Seems a shame. She'll look lovely in it too. It's got to be here somewhere.* It was. Then, shoes. Shoes had been such a problem for the past weeks—everything either too big or too small. Paulette finally gave up on finding a pair that would fit. *Well, I suppose Mary doesn't really need shoes now, does she? Now does she?...* As Paulette left, Cathy, who cleaned for Mom, arrived to do the house one last time. As the water heated for tea, we sat and talked. *Your mother always had a cup of tea waiting for me. She was the only one who ever did. Other people try to get every last drop of work out of you. Sometimes you mother just wanted me to sit.* She thought, then said with a smile—*That's harder.* As we talk, Paulette calls and says, *Your mother got a new pair of slippers for Christmas. They're somewhere on the chair next to the dresser. Send them up to Whalen's because your mother wouldn't like to be there without her shoes on, now really, would she? Would she?*

The end result is that, thanks to her friends, Mary Cain looked fine. I thought she looked very pleased with herself. Maybe because she had her shoes on.

———

When people ask *What happened?* my brother explains.

He and Mom had a good day. They talked. Mom napped. When she got up for dinner, Paul asked if he could help. She said no, she could do it, and she fixed herself a bowl of tomato soup. After dinner and the news, she said she was going to lie down for a while. Paul kept checking on her. Each time she was quiet and breathing easily until, on one visit, she looked awkward on the bed and Paul knew immediately that Mom had died. *Awkward how?* Like she tried to get up and fell backwards. No, not on the floor. Back onto the bed. She just fell back onto the pillow. Very simple. Very quiet. Very peaceful.

The consensus was that Mom's death was a blessing.

And an even greater blessing was that Paul had happened to be home with her.

———

Everybody had stories about Mom.

So, instead of a prayer service, I had people pull chairs around the open casket and tell their stories. As they did, a pattern emerged. People who had never met would interrupt one another's stories to say, *So that's who you are! I've been hearing about you for years!*

Take the brownies.

For the seven years I was directing plays at the Boston Shakespeare Company, before every opening, Mom would bake and send brownies to the cast—shoeboxes full of them. When Kevin Bradt told a story about waiting for the brownies to arrive, a woman jumped in and said, *I used to drive Mary to the Trailways Bus station to mail them,* to which Kevin answered, *Oh, you're Pat.* Then someone else said that, after a while, Mary began to bake an extra box of brownies each time for the man at Trailways who was in charge of shipping. Somebody else—who had never met him—remembered his name—*Mr. McGee.* Lots of people remembered the name of Mom's driving teacher—*Mr. Davis*—and, although none of us had ever actually met him, we knew a great deal about him—as we knew a lot about one another. It became clear that knowing Mary plugged you into a chain of friendship that included pretty much everyone she had ever known.

Paulette would say later, *Usually I'm depressed after a funeral, but this time I feel pretty good,* which is, I think, how we all felt after the wake. The stories were joyous and moving and funny and I could include more charming stories here about this good old woman who, by treating everyone as a friend, made them friends to one another—but I won't, because they weren't the real story.

The real story—which no one told because no one had noticed—was how, on the night she died, her older son, who twenty-four hours earlier had been in El Paso, Texas, was in the house with her, while her younger son, who had taken care of her for months, was having dinner that night with friends in a restaurant in New York City.

The real story was how both of her sons, thinking they were taking care of her, were actually being ruthlessly manipulated by an extremely savvy, fierce woman who still lurked inside the lovely old lady everybody was remembering.

————

After she said, *Give my love to everyone in New York,* her last words to me—and perfect—Paul drove me to the train.

I slept the six-hour train ride to the city, dropped my bag off at home, and got ready to run around town doing errands.

Before leaving the house, I called Paul to ask how things were going. He told me everything was fine and said, *Have a good time.* I hung up and started out. On a hunch, I called Paul back and asked him to do me a favor. *Check the dish on the counter by the kitchen sink. See if there are any pink pills in the dish.*

We had gone over the medications carefully, but we hadn't talked about the pink pills since Paul wouldn't have to deal with them. These were the small pills that didn't have to be mashed into food for Mom to take them. I wanted Paul to check on them because, a few days before, I had noticed untaken pink pills building up in the pill dish. When I asked Mom about them and she told me she had forgotten to take them, I got very angry. The pink pills were Mom's heart medication. *You can lay off the thyroid medication if you want, but take the heart medication. They're blood thinners and the dosage is very exact. That's why they test your blood levels every week. You have to have to have to take the heart medication.* And she responded, as with the check book, *OK, OK, Billy, just don't shout at me. . . .*

Paul returns to the phone and, assuming all is in order, says, *Yes, there are some pills there.* Knowing that things aren't in order, I tell my brother to have Mom take a pill now. Right now. He says no. When I ask why not, he says she's sleeping. When I say, *Well, wake her up,* Paul says no. She had started to have some back pain and it was too soon for morphine so she had asked for some sleeping medication and he gave it to her.

I don't say anything, but I find myself becoming irrationally angry, knowing she never takes sleeping medication in the middle of the day.

Never.

Paul asks if he did something wrong and I say, *No, it's fine*, though I don't mean it. Paul hears the disapproval under my words and starts—justifiably—to get annoyed. *Look, did you leave me in charge here or not?* I say—and mean—*You're right. You're absolutely right.*

Before I sign off, Paul tells me to relax. Everything is under control.

And everything was under control, but not his and certainly not mine.

———

People at the wake all said Mom's death was a blessing. It wasn't. Not in the sense that they meant it.

It was a plan.

Mary D. Cain, having accepted the fact that she was going to die, made a mental list that probably looked something like this:

a. Get Billy out of the house.
b. Get Paul home.
c. Die.

And that's exactly what she did.

———

The vision at the heart of the Bible can be expressed as a simple riddle: a magnificent, unapproachable God says to us, "Approach. Come closer...."

*Closer* is the impulse behind every book in the Bible.

And we were getting there. Maybe not *close* yet, but *closer*. Book by book, God moved closer—then the books end, leaving out the last two thousand years of the journey.

The Bible, though long, is incomplete.

It's time to add a new book to the Bible.

———

Before she became the lovely old lady of the stories at the wake, Mary Cain had been a fierce up-from-poverty fighter. Her energy, which had powered the family, had a take-no-prisoners quality to it that had created distance among us. It was sometimes easier and safer to love Mary Cain from a ways away. Even during the months I was taking care of her, I was still always trying to escape to New York, and Paul ... well, Paul had been around the world the hard way and had finally settled in El Paso—a significant distance away.

God in the Bible has exactly this same problem with his children.

Distance.

In fact, lessening that distance is the story of the Bible.

The difference between God and Mom, however, was that she—a mother—intended to eliminate it once and for all if it was the last thing she did. And, in a way, it had to be the last thing she did, because the only significant thing she had left to work with was her actual death.

There is, of course, no way to verify this, but I believe that once she had accepted her death, Mary Cain set out to use death itself exactly as she would have, years before, used her ironing board to iron a shirt.

She would use her death to close—once and for all—the distance she had helped to create.

———

So—she set us up.

Paul, as I said, had not been home for Dad's death. Mom was not about to let Paul be absent a second and final time. She would get Paul home for her death.

To die, she had to get me out of the house. I wouldn't let her die. Die? I wouldn't let her stop doing her checkbook.

So, she stopped taking the crucial medication—for how long, I don't know—and she offered me a trip to New York.

I leapt at it.

I called Paul.

He came and, with us thinking we were taking care of her, she had us exactly where she wanted us. Which was also where, in a perfect world, we would have wanted to be.

And we sat and we had a last supper.

———

Paul and I have absolutely no memory of what the three of us talked about that night. Just that we were happy and to-gether and we did not want to have the conversation end.

(This dinner, by the way, solved, at least for a night, my core riddle, the riddle of my priesthood—and, I suppose, all priest-hoods—how to make everything that is broken whole again.)

I left the next morning.

Paul and Mom had a day alone with one another. (I won-der when was the last time they had been alone together? Without me or Janet or Nancy or Dad? Just the two of them?)

Together, they had a day and an evening of real peace and contentment.

Then, having loved her own who were in the world and having loved them to the end—and having done absolutely everything she could—Mary Cain stopped the clock.

———

And now I ask myself the question that gets asked about all religious events from Adam and Eve to the Exodus to the Resurrection: Did it actually happen?

Was Mom doing what I think she was doing? Did my mother actually go Kübler-Ross's stages of dying one stage better and invent a new one—usefulness?

Did I really see what I think I saw?

———

I didn't at the time.

It was only later, while I was cleaning out the apartment, that individual events began to emerge as a design. Still, that doesn't prove or disprove anything. Most religious events, because they are unique, are beyond proof. Still, if you can't ask for proof, you can ask about effect. Take Exodus. Or Jesus's Resurrection. Whatever actually *happened,* people at the time felt *something* did. This isn't proof, but it is a finger pointing to a moment announcing—*something* happened here. *Whatever* actually happened, these events had an effect.

They *worked.*

And the retelling of the story continues the effect of the event—a people achieving freedom, breaking the bonds of death. Strangely, mysteriously, religiously, this works whether the event actually happened or not.

And this is part of the wonder of story.

And the story of the Bible.

Now, to apply all this to my small story—

Did what Mom was trying to do work?

And the answer is discouraging.

No, it did not work.

Not immediately.

At the time I felt that I had screwed up by being in New York.

And as for my brother...?

My brother didn't speak at the wake. He told no stories. He laughed and cried with the rest of us, but said nothing. When I ask him later why he didn't speak, he said he would have fallen apart. Besides, he said with sad acceptance, *besides, what is there to say? You kept her alive for a year. I come home and she's dead the next day.*

———

I said Mom's funeral, as I had Dad's.

There wasn't much to do to get ready for the funeral. Mom and I had talked about it beforehand. She took me by surprise when she requested that we sing the hymn "Let There Be Peace on Earth and Let It Begin with Me." I thought she was kidding, so I laughed. When she asked why, I said it seemed like an unlikely hymn for such a turbulent woman. She got offended and we had a fight about it which I thought proved my point.

Kevin Bradt—of the above brownie story, Jesuit priest, my best friend, and a very good friend of Mom's—got me through it. It was, for a funeral, a joyous affair. There was a lot of laughter, though I was the only one who laughed when the choir sang "Let There Be Peace on Earth and Let It Begin with Me," so I guess she got away with it.

———

Paul and I had a good week in Syracuse, starting to clean out the apartment.

We didn't get a lot of work done.

We had some meals.

We took some trips.

We went to Otisco Lake where Dad, Mom, Paul and I had spent the most peaceful weeks of our lives, summer after summer, at Aunt Marg's camp. We hadn't been there since we were little, and Paul and I were stunned by the beauty that—as kids—we had taken for granted.

Materially speaking, there were none of the traditional fights about who gets what. There wasn't that much to fight about. Besides, all I wanted were the family letters and photos which I promised to share. All Paul wanted was Dad's big, comfortable chair and Mom's engraved Louisville Slugger. So that worked out well.

————

We had a good week together.

Even when we were crying, we were joyous.

Then, on the last day we were together, we went down to the biggest, oldest carousel in the city, got on, and, with all the other kids waiting to wave to their parents when they appeared the next time around, we rode and rode and rode.

————

Now—and over the last ten years—whenever my brother and I have reached for an old hurt or a useful bitterness to justify some lingering family resentment, an odd thing happens.

Other memories get in the way.

The memory of *Give my love to everybody in New York.*

Paul's memory of sitting quietly though a day—a last day—with Mom.

Simple memories.

But powerful enough to eclipse the old family wounds.

The memory of the three of us at the kitchen table, late at night, talking, who knows about what.

———

Yes, it happened.

In fact, it's still happening.

And that, and not the shoes, is why, lying there in the casket, Mary Cain looked so satisfied.

———

The Bible isn't really written in words.

It's written in acts—in meals and journeys, births and deaths—and all the acts finally say the same thing.

They say *Closer. Come closer.*

That's the God part.

Closer.

Mary Cain used up everything she had—meals, journeys, her life, and even her death—so that the only thing that was left of her at the end was Closer.

———

And *that*, I think, is how you write a new book for the Bible.

*Chapter 16. How to Write a New Book for the Bible*

As I promised after the chapter "The Lost Epistle of Paul," I want to include an email that was sent to me by my friend Kevin Bradt after he read the last chapter. Kevin always could sum up what I was trying to say better than I could. You should know that Kevin was dying at the time he sent this reflection.

> *Subj: Re: thanks for everything and—*
> *Date: 12/31/2004 9:57:53 AM Pacific Standard Time*
> *From: Kmbradt*
> *To: Williampcain*
>
> *I think you should know that when I woke up this morning my mind was wholly wrapped up in your chapter. But what I want to emphasize here is the "wholly wrapped up" of my experience on waking.*
>
> *I am aware I am at peace, single, one, wholly focused, connected with an intimate part of Someone with whom I spent the night. Last night he gave his name as Pete and Mary and Mr. McGee.*
>
> *I wake wholly refreshed, moved, and in a state of single blessedness and profound gratitude.*
>
> *I realize I have walked upon this earth when I did and known these particular most "ordinary" people as part of an elaborate way of unwrapping a present, a gift given to us each day when the suns sets and we complete one more ride around the earth hurtling*

*through black space. "Oh, sooooo THAT's what was
going on all the time."*

*And this is gratitude for the WHOLE thing.*

*How lucky I've been. How blessed! And I did nothing to
be given such a wonderful gift.*

*It is one of those moments of truly grounded grace that
both roots you to the earth and all that has been and
yet launches you high into the heart of God as he
contemplates, smiles and laughs at all of us and our
cataclysmic wobbling world. "Oh good! Another one
has gotten it."*

*And I find myself smiling as I pour my orange juice and
prepare my cereal, knowing again someone is watching
me and we are close, very close.*

*And getting closer all the time.*

*Love ya — Kevin*

# 17
# *The Second Coming*

*(Though this is the last chapter in* The Book of Cain, *it was written first. It was written before I had the idea of writing a book. It was written immediately after the event described. It goes a bit beyond what I set out to do—to record the events of my parents' lives—but I offer it anyway.)*

**AUGUST 28**

It took most of a month to clean up after my parents' lives.

Every day there was less in the apartment until there was finally almost nothing. The hardest thing to throw away was the ironing board, which—since we had had it since before Paul was born—was the closest thing we had to an heirloom. Once everything else was gone, I spent another day in the empty apartment. A perfectly ordinary, slightly beat up apartment. I have trouble leaving because I know what will happen as soon as I go. And I am sorry to miss it, but I have to leave or it cannot happen.

Mom once spoke to me about Dad's visiting her after he had died. He came back to see her every now and then. Just to visit.

I suspect he will come again.

―――――

When I leave, the spirit of my mother will sit as she once did every evening.

The spirit of my mother will sit in the spirit of her rocking chair.

And Pete, her Pete, will come in.

―――――

It will become clear quickly what I didn't understand when she was telling me about Dad's visits before. I asked her then: Was he young or old. Was he like he was when he was sick or well? What was he like?

He will come in and he will be all of those things at the same time.

He will be Pete, her Pete. He will have hair. He will be bald. He will be well. He will be sick. He'll be all of those things because without any of them he would not be her Pete.

But she will be old still.

And still sick and still worrying about pain. Though the pain will never come again because pain never got to her spirit in life, so I can't believe it can touch her now that she is all spirit. I know. I said goodbye to her body. So now I say goodbye to her spirit. I pick up the ironing board—she won't be needing it; the work is finally done—and I walk out, lock the door behind me and leave her alone in the apartment.

―――――

And she is frightened to be alone.

Because it will not make sense yet to her why all the furniture is gone. All the pictures. All the stuffed animals.

But the fear will go away the moment she senses Pete standing behind her. She will grow quiet. And Pete will say *Hi, Mary. How are you?*

And she will say, *I don't really know, Pete. Something very strange is happening. Paul was here. Oh, Pete, he turned out so well! I did what you said. I took care of him the best I could. And then he took care of me. He took good care of me. He got me to sleep. It's so hard to sleep when Billy's here. He's so loud. But I don't understand about Billy.*

And Pete will laugh and say, *He always was hard to understand.*

And Mary will answer, *I know. Sometimes I think I got the wrong baby at the hospital. But this time, I don't know. Pete, he took everything out of the apartment. Everything! And then he left me with nothing. Nothing at all.*

And Pete will say, *I brought you something, Mary.*

And she will think for a long time and then she will smile because she will know what he brought.

*You brought me orchids.*

*I didn't forget this time.*

*Oh, Pete, thank you, but I don't need them anymore.*

*I know,* Pete will say, *but I wanted you to have them anyway.*

And then the spirit of my father will give the spirit of my mother the spirit of the orchids that Mary always wanted.

And suddenly they're on Bryant Avenue in the West End of Syracuse and Pete is standing at the door with flowers in his hand and a crease in his pants you could cut bread with and Mary is dressed to the nines for a dance at the

Hotel Syracuse. And, as Mary begins to become all ages at once, she says,

*Oh, Pete, I feel so strange.*

And Pete will say, *I know. Let's go for a ride.*

And with a rush of excitement, she says, *Oh, Pete. I didn't tell you! I can drive now! I can drive!*

And Pete holds out the keys to her, and she says, *No, maybe some other time.*

And they will hear music.

She will hear "I Found My Million Dollar Baby in a Five & Ten Cent Store" and he will hear something by Ethel Waters, "Heat Wave" or "His Eye Is on the Sparrow." And they will dance perfectly together, not because the songs go together but because, as Mary will remember gratefully, *Pete always was the good dancer.*

And, spinning as they used to, they will lean gracefully away from one another.

And then, at a nod from Pete, the music will slow down.

And Mary will understand.

The spinning will stop.

And they will begin to dance close.

And then they will dance closer.

Closer.

Ever closer.

# Acknowledgments

Since the writing of this book, my brother Paul has died. Like Mom and Dad, Paul died with tremendous grace.

Paul's last conscious hours were joyous. He was surrounded by his fellow teachers and his students—all trying to convince him that he was leaving a great legacy behind him after forty-two years of teaching at Ysleta High School. Paul—humble and stubborn—wasn't having it. We laughed and cried all afternoon. Mostly laughed. I know that sounds odd, but I have the pictures to prove it. Then Paul said that he could use some rest and he slept on through. A day later, surrounded by his students singing lullabies when he was restless, my brother Paul died.

Sylvia Rendon, his last principal, proved him wrong about his legacy by championing the naming of a new building after him—the Paul F. Cain Arts Center. Many people looked after Paul when he was sick. Let his best friend, Jaime Pena, and his former students—now distinguished teachers themselves, Holly Garza and Adriana Garcia—stand for them all.

Kevin Bradt , SJ, whose email is included in this book, insisted—sometimes harshly—that I finish writing the book whenever I stalled. His brother, Jack, was an ever enthusiastic supporter and a gifted listener.

Greg Boyle, SJ read early drafts and was unfailingly loving in his response. As were Tim Goley, Jairo Guzman, Wade Pizarro, and Tim Lambert. Sr. Mary Galeone, RSM, became a good friend with Mary Cain via telephone. As did Miriam Healy and so many others. Gratitude also to everyone at the Boston Shakespeare Company—including Grey Johnson, Cathy Rust, Khorshed Dubash, Steve Aveson, Charlie Marz, Jim Kitendaugh, Peter McLoughlin, Marjorie Tucker, Norman Frisch—to whom Mary Cain sent brownies for every opening night. Thanks to David and Arla Manson for constant love and support and to my assistant, Deniz Himmetoglu.

This book was performed widely as the play *How To Write a New Book for the Bible* starting at Berkeley Rep, directed by Kent Nicholson and starring Linda Gehringer, Leo Marks, Aaron Blakely, and Tyler Pierce. It was workshopped at the Ojai Playwrights Conference with Robert Egan, artistic director, Hal Brooks as director, Beth Blickers as agent and starring Patrick J. Adam—all of whom generously and wisely helped shape the telling of the story.

Thanks to Celine Allen and Robert Ellsberg. It is an honor to be published by Orbis.

Finally, thanks to Nancy—Paul's daughter—to whom all the stories now belong.

And gratitude forever to my brother, Paul F. Cain, my dad, Paul ("Pete") Cain, and my mother, Mary Dawson Cain.

Till soon.